Mosy U. Madugba

Elders

at the

Gates

With related teachings during the 4th International Ministries/Christian Leaders Prayer and Leadership Conference, "Nigeria 2000" by Emeka Nwankpa and Uduak Udofia

Spiritual Life Outreach Publication

Port Harcourt, Nigeria

Copyright © 2000 by: Mosy U. Madugba

Updated: March 2002

2ND Update 2013

April 2017 Title changed to Elders At The Gates

ISBN – **978-9783559455**

All rights reserved. No part of this book should be reproduced or transmitted in any form or by any means, electronic or mechanical, including photocopying, recording, or by any information storage and retrieval system without written permission from the Publisher.

Unless otherwise stated, all Scripture quotations are taken from The Kings James Version (KJV) of the Bible.

ELDERS AT THE GATES

Typeset and published in the Federal Republic of Nigeria by **Spiritual Life Outreach Inc.** - a multinational evangelistic/missionary Christian Organization working in several countries in Africa and some parts of the world to bring the gospel to the un-reached people-groups and mobilizing prayer efforts within the global Church.

All Trade orders to:
Outreach Christian Book Centres, #3 Babbe Street. D/Line,
P. O. Box 7960, Port Harcourt, Nigeria.
Email:revmadugba@yahoo.com
Or gcmadugba@yahoo.com
Tel:+234-907-999-0000+234-803-470-9941,+234-803-362-6795.

Printed in the Federal Republic of Nigeria

"**The elders have ceased gathering at the gate, and the young men from their music. The joy of our heart has ceased; our dance has turned into 'mourning'. The crown has fallen from our head. Woe to us, for we have sinned! Because of this our heart is faint; Because of Mount Zion (our city) which is desolate, with foxes walking about on it**"
(Lamentation 5:14-18)

"The great and noble are identified by the persons, visions, projects, and the causes they identified with and not by how much money or wealth they possess or positions they occupy nor by their age".
- The author

CONTENTS

Foreword	5
Appreciation	7
Chapter One Who is a Christian Elder?	8
Chapter Two How the Elders function in the New	22
Chapter Three More function of the City Elders for Today	30
Chapter Four How to set up an Elders Forum in a City Qualifications Summarized	46
Chapter Five Gates	58
Chapter Six Types of Gates	76
Chapter Seven Battles At The Gates	98
Chapter Eight How to Bring Healing to the Land	112
Chapter Nine Elders at the Gate: Barrister Emeka Nwankpa	120
Questions and answers	154
Chapter Ten City Eldership and Prophetic Presbytery **Ben Uduak Udofia**	166
References	185

FOREWORD

The Ministers Prayer Network in Port Harcourt was holding her normal monthly teaching, training, prayer and fasting meeting during the second quarter of 1998 when God began to speak to us about the need for the Elders in the household of faith to take their rightful places at the "City Gates", keep watch over the land, break satanic ancient altars, give spiritual directions to the body of Christ in emerging life issues. At that very time, there arose a disturbing and protracted civil strike action by civil servants in the city of Port Harcourt. Some members of Port Harcourt House of Prayer joined to encourage one of the foremost Christian Elders in our city to convene a meeting of all church leaders, from various sectors of life to pray and give a godly direction in the state.

The outcome of that gathering turned the political and social climate of Rivers State as well as Nigeria around for good. Many other cities in Nigeria began to call my office on phone to find out how they can gather their key leaders to do what we had done in Port Harcourt. The corporate prayers offered in this city went further to affect the religious tone of politics in Nigeria at that time because of one of the publications the Christian Elders in Port Harcourt made in one of the National dailies – The punch. This little book is therefore written to answer some of the questions we have been asked since then and to explain the persons, the place, the power and the roles of God's elders in a city or nation. Since it is not exhaustive in itself, I hope it will provoke more studies and findings on the subject.

Elders At The Gates

APPRECIATION

If not for God, writing this book in this season it would have been very impossible. I thank Him. I am grateful to the leadership of Port Harcourt House of Prayer, and the leadership of Rivers State Christian Elders Forum. For this updated version, Mrs Onyinye Onunka, Mr Anozie Ike, Miss Chioma Onyemachi and Miss Uju Chimbo worked really hard to get it out. Mr. Fidelis Igoni updated the cover page. Except for the Lord, my dear wife still excelled above all.

Thanks to you all

CHAPTER ONE

WHO IS A CHRISTIAN ELDER?

When we speak of Christian Elders at the city gates we refer to men and women of God (not boys and girls) who are blood washed, sanctified and filled with the Holy Spirit. These must be men of integrity whose lives are dedicated to God as an offering in righteousness. Often these are men who have by their personal knowledge and experience with God known the mind of God on general and specific issues and are committed to walking with God on a daily basis. They must be long enough in the faith to be spiritually mature and knowledgeable in the scriptures, to teach others about our faith and the principles that represent the keys of the kingdom. As tested disciples, they not only know the manners and customs of the kingdom but proclaim the same by their lifestyle. They have lived long enough in the house that they know all the corners and can take a stranger around. They must be people whom we can say have been circumcised in the foreskin of their hearts, from whom various forms of superficialities, sensual coatings, and childishness in spiritual matters have been cut off.

> *In Him you were also circumcised with the circumcision made without hands, by putting off the body of the sins of the flesh, by the circumcision of Christ. (Colossians 2:11-12)*

In the words of Paul to Timothy in 2 Timothy 3:17b; *"They are men who are thoroughly furnished unto all good works".*

These elders shine only after they have been purged of the things that are capable of reducing potential gold to clay or wood useful only for dishonorable tasks.

> *Therefore, if anyone cleanses himself from the latter, he will be a vessel for honor, sanctified and useful for the Master, prepared for every good work. (2 Tim 2:21-22)*

Although they may be drawn from various professions; one thing is common in them all: they have wisdom, which they have developed with age, reading, experience, exposure and wide interaction.

By calling, they could be Apostles, Evangelists, Prophets, Teachers, Pastors, and heads of denominations or ministries. Often you have among them successful businessmen or women, lawyers, medical personnel, civil servants and even retired Civil Servants. Among them also are active housewives. They could come from the Police or Military or Judiciary. They could be active government officials or retired persons who are no longer distracted by jobs outside the home.

Not Local Church Elders

The leaders who qualify for this office are not necessarily the local church elders ordained by local assemblies with varying criteria. The divine position of the city elders is older than the church. They have been and are still the strength of any throne or monarchy. It is instructive to note that around the Holy and most exalted throne of God are twenty-four Elders. The place of a city eldership is not won by votes and is not to be open for all. It is for those who over the years have maintained an exemplary successful Christian lifestyle and leadership, whose testimonies concerning their marriages, business life, and activities in their local churches and native communities, edify and inspire others to do more for the glory of God.

Qualifications

Maturity in the faith attested to by all is the basic criteria for qualification. A local adage says, "if a child washes his hands well, he eats with the elders". A young man or woman who may be useful to the elders in carrying out their assignment could be invited and involved. Every member has to be selected. If not selected, he waits for his turn without fermenting trouble. Moses selected the elders. They are always selected and called to the office of city eldership. There may be gray-haired people who may not be selected, not because they are not good but because not everybody must be invited to sit at the city Gate at the same time. It is simply another forum to continue to serve God and the people. They need not be ordained elders by any local church. Neither does the ordination of a believer by his local church as an elder qualify that believer automatically to be a city elder or function as one of the elders at the state gates or national gates. The spiritual tasks handled sometimes at the gates are not such that ignorant or untrained, young, good churchmen should be exposed to. Why? Simply because these tasks involve strategic level spiritual warfare which requires spiritual stamina and discipline. As a man is, so is his strength. Battles are won or lost at these gates. So you do not bring people there to make them feel good and important. It is not a political or social gathering but purely a forum for enacting strong spiritual legislation, receiving and implementing the divine purposes and plans of God over geopolitical areas and the people who live there.

The Wycliffe Bible Dictionary edited by Charles E. Pfeiffer, Howard E. Vos and John Rea explains that "the Hebrew term *zaqen* which is interpreted elder, does not necessarily mean an old man, but does imply one of maturity and experience, who has assumed leadership among his own Kinsmen and in his town or tribe (Numbers 11:16).

> *So, the LORD said to Moses: "Gather to Me seventy men of the elders of Israel, whom you know to be the elders of the people and officers over them; bring them to the tabernacle of meeting, that they may stand there with you.*

Although the elders were not elected, during most of the periods from Moses to Ezra and on into the intertestamental era; they were recognized as the highest authoritative body over the people. The term *zaqen* in Hebrew is the equivalent to the Homeric *gerontes*, the Spartan (Greek) *prebys*, the Roman *senatus* (from where we get the root word for senators), and the Arab "sheikh".

During the time of the Judges, God chose women like Deborah to sit at city and national Gates, as Elders. The word "Elder" is not synonymous with the male gender – Judges 4:5 NKJV clearly shows that Deborah as an Elder at the national Gates of Israel, did a good job of judging the people and giving them direction in a period of national emergency.

> *And she would sit under the palm tree of Deborah between Ramah and Bethel in the mountains of Ephraim. And the children of Israel came up to her for judgment.*

The existence of the elder's place dates back to pre-Israel times. The Elders system existed in Egypt (Genesis 50:7 NKJV).

> *And Joseph went up to bury his father: and with him went up all the servants of Pharaoh, the elders of his house, and all the elders of the land of Egypt.*

Psalm 105:22 (RSV); in Moab and Midian (Numbers 22: 4, 7) and in Gibeon (Joshua 9:11).

Functions From The Old Testament

(a) God's contact point

The 'elders of Israel', first heard of in Exodus 3:16-18, were assembled by Moses to receive God's announcement of liberation from Egypt.

> *Go and gather the elders of Israel together, and say unto them, The LORD God of your fathers, the God of Abraham, of Isaac, and of Jacob, appeared unto me, saying, I have surely visited you, and seen that which is done to you in Egypt: And I have said, I will bring you up out of affliction of Egypt unto the land of Canaanites, and the Hittites, and the Amorites, and the Pizzities, and the Hivites and the Jebusites, unto a land flowing with milk and honey. And they shall hearken to thy voice: and thou shalt come, thou and the elders of Israel, unto the King of Egypt, and ye shall say to him, The LORD God of the Hebrews hath met with us: and now let us go, we beseech thee, three days' journey into the wilderness, that we may sacrifice to the Lord our God." (Exo. 3:16 – 18)*

When God has a message for the people, he looks for and assembly of elders to deliver it (See also Ezekiel 8: 1 – 3, 6 – 18 NKJV).

> *And it came to pass in the sixth year, in the sixth month, on the fifth day of the month, as I sat in my house with the elders of Judah sitting before me, that the hand of the Lord GOD fell upon me there. Then I looked, and there was a likeness,*

like the appearance of fire — from the appearance of His waist and downward, fire; and from His waist and upward, like the appearance of brightness, like the color of amber. He stretched out the form of a hand and took me by a lock of my hair; and the Spirit lifted me up between earth and heaven, and brought me in visions of God to Jerusalem, to the door of the north gate of the inner court, where the seat of the image of jealousy was, which provokes to jealousy.

(b) God's earthly witnesses

God's covenant was ratified at Mount Sinai in the presence of 70 of the elders of Israel (Exodus 24: 1, 9, 14; cf. 19:7). These were the 'nobles' as King James Version refers to them or the chief men of the nation (Exodus 24:11). They were national elders. Every country needs them. I visited Abidjan in Ivory Coast and was hosted by one such Elder. He is a believer in Christ who wrote the first Constitution of the country and still chaired the Constitution Review Committee in the year 2000. He is Mr. Mathien Ekra and is referred to as the 'Grand mediateur de la republique de Côte d'Ivoire'. It does not matter what the problem is at any given point in time. When he speaks the nation listens. We need more of them.

(c) Provide leadership to the people

Seventy elders were specially anointed with the Spirit to aid Moses in governing the nation (Num. 11:16 – 25).

> *So the LORD said to Moses: "Gather to Me seventy men of the elders of Israel, whom you know to be the elders of the people and officers over them; bring them to the tabernacle of meeting, that they may stand there with you. Then I will come down and talk with you there. I will take of the Spirit that is upon you and will put the same upon them; and they shall bear the burden of the people with you, that you may not bear it yourself alone. Then you shall say to the people, 'Consecrate yourselves for tomorrow, and you shall eat meat; for you have wept in the hearing of the LORD, saying, "Who will give us meat to eat? For it was well with us in Egypt." Therefore, the LORD will give you meat, and you shall eat. You shall eat, not one day, nor two days, nor five days, nor ten days, nor twenty days, but for a whole month, until it comes out of your nostrils and becomes loathsome to you, because you*

have despised the LORD who is among you, and have wept before Him, saying, "Why did we ever come up out of Egypt? And Moses said, "The people whom I am among are six hundred thousand men on foot; yet You have said, 'I will give them meat, that they may eat for a whole month.' Shall flocks and herds be slaughtered for them, to provide enough for them? Or shall all the fish of the sea be gathered together for them, to provide enough for them?" And the LORD said to Moses, "Has the LORD's arm been shortened? Now you shall see whether what I say will happen to you or not." So Moses went out and told the people the words of the LORD, and he gathered the seventy men of the elders of the people and placed them around the tabernacle. Then the LORD came down in the cloud, and spoke to him, and took of the Spirit that was upon him, and placed the same upon the seventy elders; and it happened, when the Spirit rested upon them, that they prophesied, although they never did so again.

(d) Lead in community intercession over serious matters

Whenever the community sins against God and God threatens to bring judgment, the elders of the congregation or community were the ones who represented the people in making atonement.

Now if the whole congregation of Israel sins unintentionally, and the thing is hidden from the eyes of the assembly, and they have done something against any of the commandments of the LORD in anything which should not be done and are guilty; when the sin which they have sinned becomes known, then the assembly shall offer a young bull for the sin, and bring it before the tabernacle of meeting. And the elders of the congregation shall lay their hands on the head of the bull before the Lord. Then the bull shall be killed before the Lord (Levi. 4:13 – 15).

Whatever agreement they had with God was binding on all the people.

(e) King makers

When Samuel served as Judge and Prophet of Israel, the authority of the elders was in principle greater than that of the King. The

King could not make serious decisions without consulting the elders (2 Kings 23:1). It was this group, which demanded that Samuel appoint a King (1 Sam. 8:4-6), and as a group, they were party to the royal covenant, which established David as King (2 Samuel 5:3). Out of the council of Elders (*gerousia*) of the Hellenistic period in Judah developed the Great Assembly (Knesset) of the Jews which in 142BC granted great power to Simon the Maccabean leader (1 Macc. 14:28). The Great Sanhedrin with its 71 members, the supreme legislative body prior to A.D. 70 was the ultimate form of the institution of the 'Elders of Israel'.

(f) A rallying point in moments of crisis

In Babylon while in exile, the elders were the focal point of the Jewish Community (Jeremiah 29: 1, Ezekiel 8:1; 14:1; 20: 1-5), and after the return to Jerusalem they continued to give active leadership (Ezra 5:5,9; 6:7-8,14; 10:8,14).

> *Now these are the words of the letter that Jeremiah the prophet send from Jerusalem unto the residue of the elders which were carried away captives, and to the priests, and to the prophets, and to all the people whom Nebuchadnezzar had carried away captive from Jerusalem to Babylon;" (Jer. 29:1 NKJV)*

Now some of the elders of Israel came to me and sat before me. (Ezekiel 14:1)

It came to pass in the seventh year, in the fifth month, on the tenth day of the month, that certain of the elders of Israel came to inquire of the LORD and sat before me. Then the word of the LORD came to me, saying, "Son of man, speak to the elders of Israel, and say to them, 'Thus says the Lord GOD: "Have you come to inquire of Me? As I live," says the Lord GOD, "I will not be inquired of by you."' Will you judge them, son of man, will you judge them? Then make known to them the abominations of their fathers. "Say to them, 'Thus says the Lord GOD: "On the day when I chose Israel and raised My hand in an oath to the descendants of the house of Jacob and made Myself known to them in the land of Egypt, I raised My hand in an oath to them, saying, 'I am the LORD your God. (Ezekiel 20:1-5)

Elders At The Gates

CHAPTER TWO

HOW THE ELDERS FUNCTIONED IN THE NEW TESTAMENT CHURCH

The concept of Elders also existed in the New Testament church. In this dispensation the elders played the following roles:

(a) They Administered Relief

They are godly and have wisdom to selflessly administer donated relief materials to people who actually need help righteously without tribal or ethnic sentiments and partiality. By doing this they took care of the less privileged in the society.

Then the disciples, every man according to his ability, determined to send relief unto the brethren which dwelt in Judea: Which also they did, and sent it to the elders by the hands of Barnabas and Saul. (Acts 11: 29 – 30).

(b) Corrected Errors

Truly *mature* and *well-informed* elders, who have lasted long and have been consistent in the faith, are custodians of sound Biblical doctrine and tradition of heaven handed over to us by Christ and the earliest Apostles. These are they who teach the younger members by their own examples virtues and godly lifestyle.

*And when they were come to Jerusalem, they were received of the church, and of the apostles and **elders**, and they declared all things that God had done with them: And the apostles and **elders** came together for to consider of this matter: And they wrote letters by them after this manner; The apostle and **elders** and brethren send greeting unto the brethren which are of the Gentiles in Antioch and Syria and Cilicia (Acts 15:4, 6, 23).*

And the things that you have heard from me among many witnesses, commit these to faithful men who will be able to teach others also. (2 Tim 2:2-2)

(c) Hold Fast The Faithful Word

Young ones are easier to be swayed. They have not proved a lot of things. So whatever looks exciting and entertaining they reason, must be good.

For this reason, I left you in Crete, that you should set in order the things that are lacking, and appoint elders in every city as

I commanded you: Holding fast the faithful word as he has been taught, that he may be able, by sound doctrine, both to exhort and convict those who contradict."(Titus 1:5, 9 NKJV)

(d) **Rule Well In The Body Of Christ**
Let the elders that rule well be counted worthy of double honor, especially they who labor in the word and doctrine (1 Timothy 5:17)

(e) **Minister Healing To The Sick**

In the New Testament, the elders are expected to provide leadership and to watch over the flock of God so things will not go wrong. They should study the word and provide sound teachings, ministering healing to the sick.

Is anyone among you sick? Let him call for the elders of the church, and let them pray over him, anointing him with oil in the name of the Lord; And the prayer of faith will save the sick and the Lord will raise him up; And if he has committed any sins he will be forgiven (James 5:14,15).

No matter how many places a young man has traveled to, the number of people he has preached to, the large congregation he has built up or the money in his bank account, such do not bestow on him the spiritual authority of the aged, who are spiritually exercised in administering Godly Counsel and words of wisdom. They make decrees, which heaven honors and hell submits to. It is helpful to note that in heaven, God has surrounded Himself not with glamorous and ostentatious rich young men, but with Elders. It is pitiful to observe today in several local churches, how easily babies in the Lord are made elders because they are rich and have political influence in the land.

Irrespective of our profession, vocation, social or economic status, a spiritual infant must be given the chance to grow into spiritual adulthood before being allowed to rule. Some of these hasty ordinations destroy the ordained while some of them bring reproach to the name and work of the Lord. A zealous but untutored baby elder in a position of great responsibility is like a novice handling poisonous chemicals in a laboratory. Because he has no idea how to function in the laboratory, he can only bring harm to himself. At best, the acid he would produce, (like the anointing of the Holy Spirit without sound wisdom and righteous living) will corrode and harm him and all those he is carrying along.

Spiritually immature people or baby elders are capable of doing great harm to the body of Christ because they are not allowed to go through several vital spiritual developmental stages that could have strengthened and fortified their spiritual foundation to enable them carry heavy spiritual responsibilities successfully.

It takes only nine months (¾ of a year) to conceive and put to bed a baby. But is takes eighteen (18) solid years to nurture a child to adulthood and sometimes even at eighteen; some adults are still not mature enough to be independent.

The same principle applies to new converts in the body of Christ. Those for milk should be allowed to drink enough of it before being introduced to solid food. If a child is malnourished, it shows in his stunted growth. We have several spiritually malnourished adults leading in many local churches, and some of them even function as pastors of large congregations today. It ought not to be so.

(f) Kingdom Fathers

Godly Christian elders are to provide parental guidance to the younger ones. To get the required parental counsel from them, the younger people would need to accord them their due respect. Producing a generation of spiritual bastards is not the best for the Church in any nation. We must make use of the elders in the body.

Before I conclude this subsection, I want to point out a subtle snare Satan has placed on the path of many young believers today. Somehow people just do not have respect for elders any more. This is a dangerous trend. And we must heed Apostle Paul's admonition to Timothy his disciple, saying:

> *Do not rebuke an older man, but exhort him as a father, the younger men as brothers, the older women as mothers, the younger girls as sisters, with all purity. Do not receive an accusation against an elder except from two or three witnesses* (1 Timothy 5: 1-2).

Apostle Peter also echoes these sentiments when he said,

> *Likewise, you younger people, submit yourselves to your elders. Yes, all of you be submissive to one another, and be clothed with humility, for "God resists the proud, but gives grace to the humble."* (1 Peter 5:5)

(g) The church's representatives in heaven

Feiffer, Vos and Rea wrote: "In this vision of heaven, John saw twenty-four Elders seated upon the thrones surrounding the throne of God, clothed in white garments and wearing golden crowns (Revelations 4:4). They fall down in worship and cast their crowns before God's throne (Revelation 4:10, cf. 11:16, 19:4), and with their harps and bowls of incense, symbolizing the prayers of the saints; they sing a new song to the Lamb (Revelation 5:8-10). As elders, they represent God's people; their thrones and crowns symbolize a Kingly role, while their acts of worship and bowls of incense suggest a Priestly function. Thus they seem to be the chief representatives of the redeemed as a Kingdom of Priests (Revelation 1:6; cf. 20:6, 1 Peter 2:5, Exodus 19:6)".

(h) A forum for resolving conflicts and trying civil cases (Mathew 26:3-5, 59-60).

Whenever serious conflicts and problems arose in the land of Israel especially those with the potential of causing unrest in the land, the Elders were quickly informed. This principle is applied everywhere human beings live today. It is practiced in our rural communities. It is practiced in politics. They have the wealth of experiences and cumulative wisdom gathered over the cumulative years they have spent on earth, which helps to provide quicker solutions and direction to every generation. Where godly and spiritually mature elders meet regularly to handle these matters and take necessary actions in line with the word of God and the leading of Holy Spirit, the corrupt and devilish ones will not have their way to misdirect the people. Justice and equity will thrive and the oppressed will be relieved. God will be pleased and will bless and favor the people. But when the wicked and ungodly one's man the gates, hell is let loose and iniquity will abound.

Read what the Titled religious but wicked Leaders did to Jesus Christ – the Savior.

And it came to pass, when Jesus had finished all these sayings, he said unto his disciples, Ye know that after two days is the feast of Passover, and the Son of man is betrayed to be crucified. Then assembled together the chief priest, and the scribes and the elders of the people unto the palace of the high priest, who was called "Caiaphas" (Mathew 26:3-5, 59-60)

CHAPTER THREE

MORE FUNCTIONS OF THE CITY ELDERS FOR TODAY

1. **Keep Spiritual Surveillance**
They keep spiritual surveillance over the cities – Job 1:5, John 7:6-7. They listen to news on the radio, watch the television news; read newspapers and pick vital information for prayer purposes. Where they see obscene films on the TV, they call the attention of those in charge, where they pick up signals indicating that a devilish group is planning to come to their city to have a meeting, they make quick moves to stop that from taking place. Informed elders sensitize the people to do away with ungodly festivals and traditions that spiritually pollute and bring curses and divine judgment on the land. They notice when occult groups start entering their city and expel them by prayer and prophetic actions. They notice when ungodly bills are being processed to be passed into Law and make all necessary efforts to stop them. Where such laws already exist, they initiate moves to repeal such laws and follow such moves through.

2. Spiritual Legislation

They make spiritual legislation over the territories they watch over. Where the need arises, they make conclusive prophetic pronouncements.

"This decision is by the decree of the watchers and the sentence by the word of the holy ones, in order that the living may know that the Most High reigns in the kingdom of men" (Dan. 4: 17).

"Assuredly I say to you, whatever you bind on earth will be bound in heaven and whatever you loose on earth will be loosed in heaven" (Matthew 18:18) (refers to church leadership) John 20:22 – 23.

3. Call Forth Redemptive Gifts

They identify and call forth redemptive gifts of the people. Redemptive gifts are the God given talents, skills, and mineral and other natural resources of a people group, which is localized for their survival and sustenance. These are meant to be exploited for the social and economic uplifting of the people. When a people live in rebellion against God, the land may refuse to yield her increase, and the rain be withheld. The people may study and make efforts to escape obscurity and come to the limelight; but the results show that they burn all their energy to achieve little or nothing. When the *Elders at the City Gate* reconcile with God, they, like Elijah, can bring the rains and perform similar feats like Joshua at Gilgal. They are at liberty to call forth to manifest all hidden and "invisible" varieties of corn in the land. Suddenly, the people who were noted for nothing good begin to arise, blossom and shine. We may recall that Joshua's act of obedience at Gilgal changed the spiritual and social status of Israel and made the land to yield her corn. (Joshua 5: 9-12) They did not need anymore 'manna.' Manna is a blessing that has no name, that lasts for only half a day, a blessing that could not make anyone rich because it could not be stored.

The elders in Rivers State, Nigeria have in the past counseled and helped the different Governors of this State to remove offensive immoral statues and replace them with godly ones, stop some ungodly festivals, despite the argument by some that such festivals generate some money for the State. Hotel Presidential, the foremost five-star Hotel in the City named her restaurant "Mermaid" restaurant. It was changed to "Rivers" restaurant by a Christian Governor. Many other strategic changes also took place in the state which I cannot mention in this book. The elders handled some matters with prayer and sometimes came into hot rebukes to get the then Governor to understand their spiritual stand and co-operate. Each city needs such elders.

4. Godly Unity

Laying foundations for godly unity by being supportive of each other and generating healing for all broken relationships. Some people unite to do evil, plan wickedness against other successful fellows. The godly leaders discharge this. They know that a kingdom divided against itself cannot stand; so they do not encourage fights against one another in the Kingdom of God. No genuine Godly Elder will get involved in this.

5. Generational Ministers

Elders promote generational ministries by developing a succession of well-trained leaders and ministers. A godly parent invests in the education and development of his children. Good city or national elders are not selfish. They invest and set up the necessary framework for developing better quality future leaders.

6. Spiritual Direction

Give spiritual direction to the church, the people and the government - e.g. (Ezra 3:10-13).

When the builders laid the foundation of the temple of the LORD, *the priests stood in their apparel with trumpets, and the Levites, the sons of Asaph, with cymbals, to praise the* LORD, *according to the ordinance of David king of Israel. And they sang responsively, praising and giving thanks to the* LORD: *"For He is good, for His mercy endures forever toward Israel. Then all the people shouted with a great shout, when they praised the* LORD, *because the foundation of the house of the* LORD *was laid. But many of the priests and Levites and heads of the fathers' houses, old men who had seen the first temple, wept with a loud voice when the foundation of this temple was laid before their eyes. Yet many shouted aloud for joy, so that the people could not discern the noise of the shout of joy from the noise of the weeping of the people, for the people shouted with a loud shout, and the sound was heard afar off."*

Many people see things on the surface. A practical example was demonstrated in Rivers State in 1998. During the election campaign for the Governorship of Rivers State, the elders at the gate who had been praying and watching over the city, (Port Harcourt, Nigeria) met regularly to pray. When the parties chose their candidates, one party chose a Roman Catholic Knight as their candidate; the other party chose a Spiritist. The elders prayed and invited the one they could identify with and led him to Christ. The same day, they anointed and dedicated him as a governor of the state ahead of time. They presented him before the Lord. Though his opponent had gained more grounds, as he had at that time gotten the political pillars and various shakers and movers in different facets of the society to his side using gifts and money, the *Elders* and the *Intercessors* traveled to various parts of the state and dealt with things that needed to be dealt with in prayer. Newspaper Publications were made on National Dailies and letters distributed to give the church a direction at the moment. The non – churchgoers also saw the point the elders were making. Despite the high- level sorcery and political connections employed by the opposite camp, the spiritist candidate lost. What the *Elders at the Gate* did at that moment, no other existing body was in a position to do and could do. Why? They dealt decisively with the cosmic powers that controlled the throne, wresting the authority to hand the place back to God.

Though the *Elders at the Gates* are not politicians, they take side with God to safeguard the land from satanic invasion and pollution. They alert the people about certain things and help give direction for the peace and good of the land. Anyone who grew up in a typical rural African Community would have noticed that the satanic elders at the gates notice when actions and events which defy the satanic sacredness of the land occur and they quickly cry foul insisting that the land has been defiled. They would go to the shrines and on the altars of Satan to make sacrifices and atonement. Once any of them notices it, he will contact the others. The people are also educated about these things so that when they notice such forbidden things done anywhere, they quickly run to the elders. Where are God's own elders? Are they together? What influence do they have in your locality?

The society is decaying, the youths are going crazy, and blood is spilled daily, the church's standards are personalized and lowered. No group of elders come up to jointly and persistently hold workshops, seminars and teachings to restore biblical standards, why? Are our Christian elders themselves culprits? Is it possible that they are overtaken and carried away?

7. Identify and Destroy Evil Altars

Identify and destroy evil altars and idolatrous traditions and establish godly ones.

> *Again proclaim, saying, "Thus says the LORD of hosts:" My cities shall again spread out through prosperity; The LORD will again comfort Zion, And will again choose Jerusalem. Then I raised my eyes and looked, and there were four horns. And I said to the angel who talked with me, "What are these? "So he answered me," These are the horns that have scattered Judah, Israel, and Jerusalem." Then the LORD showed me four craftsmen. And I said, "What are these coming to do? "So he said, "These are the horns that scattered Judah, so that no one could lift up his head; but the craftsmen* are coming to terrify them, to cast out the horns of the nations that lifted up their horn against the land of Judah to scatter it. (Zechariah 1: 17 – 21)*

There are all sort of idolatrous festivals and masquerades taking place in our communities strengthening Satan's grip on the land and weakening the effect of the church and slowing down the growth of God's kingdom. If we have Godly Elders in the communities, why have they not risen to stop these evil practices started in ignorance?

8. Spiritual Parents

Elders give spiritual parental care to the younger generation in the body. According to 1 Peter 5: 1 – 2, they provide mentoring services.

The elders who are among you I exhort, I who am a fellow elder and a witness of the sufferings of Christ, and also a partaker of the glory that will be revealed: Shepherd the flock of God which is among you, serving as overseers, not by compulsion but willingly, not for dishonest gain but eagerly.

9. Doctrinal Clearing House

Elders act as a clearinghouse on doctrinal issues:

Acts 15: 2, *"...they determined that Paul and Barnabas, and certain other of them, should go up to Jerusalem unto the **apostles** and **elders** about this question'* (Note "...and the elders...")

10. Identify And Break Curses

They identify and break curses plaguing their land.

Then Joshua charged them at that time, saying," Cursed be the man before the LORD who rises up and builds this city Jericho; he shall lay its foundation with his firstborn, and with his youngest he shall set up its gates. (Joshua 6:26)

In his days Hiel of Bethel built Jericho. He laid its foundation with Abiram his firstborn, and with his youngest *son* Segub he set up its gates, according to the word of the LORD, which He had spoken through Joshua the son of Nun." **(***1 Kings 16: 34)*

Then the men of the city said to Elisha, "Please notice, the situation of this city is pleasant, as my lord sees; but the water is bad, and the ground barren." And he said, "Bring me a new bowl, and put salt in it." So they brought it to him. Then he went out to the source of the water, and cast in the salt there, and said, "Thus says the LORD: 'I have healed this water; from it there shall be no more death or barrenness.'" (2 Kings 2:19-22)

Prayers
- Pray to enter your city in the spirit and see its spiritual state the way God sees it.

- Pray to take control over all powers of darkness
- Pray to sack all the ungodly elders at the gates who give ungodly counsel and raise satanic altars.
- Deal with satanic gatekeepers who resist the establishment of genuine vibrant churches and try to kill true prophets in the city.
- Pray to bring forth godly city elders for your city
- Pray that the heaven over your city be opened

Ezekiel demonstrated this in Ezekiel 9:1-2,

> *Then He called out in my hearing with a loud voice, saying, "Let those who have charge over the city draw near, each with a deadly weapon in his hand." And suddenly six men came from the direction of the upper gate, which faces north, each with his battle-axe in his hand. One man among them was clothed with linen and had a writer's inkhorn at his side. They went in and stood beside the bronze altar."*

In the New Testament, local assemblies or churches as we call them today or denominations in a larger sense, appointed and ordained elders to help in overseeing the work of the ministry. By hierarchy, they were not lower in ranking to any other officer in the church. The issue of who is higher in authority is a denominational arrangement. Apostle Peter referred to himself as a church elder. (1 Peter 5: 1). These offices were created for service and not to empower anyone to flex his muscle of religious authority over others. Quest for these powers are clear indications of a life more controlled by the lust of the flesh than by the Holy Spirit. Such are babies and are of very limited usefulness at the gates.

In such churches like the one in Ephesus, where Paul spent years working, there could have been a "resident pastor" with elder Paul in their midst. In this situation, who had the leadership authority? Part of what God is doing in this new millennium is to fundamentally restructure and reform our religious mentalities. Some of the teachings we have copied from the traditions of men, swallowed hook line and sinker and taught in Bible Colleges will be reformed and radically restructured by God in the present apostolic era.

Elders At The Gates

Elders At The Gates

CHAPTER FOUR

HOW TO SET UP AN ELDERS FORUM IN A CITY

Where there are no Christian Elders in a city, something very vital is lacking. Paul wrote addressing such a situation in Titus 1:5

> *For this reason, I left you in Crete that you set in order the things that are lacking and appoint elders in every city as I commanded you.*

Intercessors for the land should call forth God fearing elders in prayer.

> *In a great house there are not only vessels of gold or silver, but also of wood and of earth, and some to honor and some to dishonor. If a man therefore **purges** himself (which men really find difficult to do) from these he shall be a vessel unto honor, sanctified (divinely set aside) and meet (good enough) for the Master's use and prepared unto every good work 2 Tim. 2: 20-21.*

Call forth through intense prayers purged and refined godly men to man the spiritual gates of your city.

You cannot do without them.

Qualifications Summarized

Anyone called to function in that Eldership Council:

- Must be genuinely born again - a certified regenerated child of God.
- Filled with the Holy Spirit, evidenced by the richness of the fruit of the Holy Spirit – love, joy, peace, longsuffering, kindness, goodness, faithfulness, gentleness and self-control. They must not only claim to have the fruit of the spirit, but their daily lives must profoundly manifest this fruit.

    And those who are in Christ have crucified the flesh with its passions and desires. If we live in the Spirit, let us also walk in the spirit. Let us not become conceited, provoking one another, envying one another. (Gal. 5: 24-26).

- Must be properly followed up and solidly discipled.
- Must have been long and consistent in the faith.
- Must have a generally acceptable testimony as one who is *"thoroughly furnished unto good works"* (2 Timothy 3: 17)

- Must be endowed with Godly wisdom – Some have abundance of earthly divisive wisdom.
  Who is wise and understanding among you? Let him show by good conduct that his works are done in the meekness of wisdom. But if you have bitter envy and self-seeking in your hearts, do not boast against the truth. This wisdom does not descend from above, but is earthly, sensual and demonic. For where envy and self – seeking exists, confusion and every evil thing will be there. But the wisdom that is from above is first, pure, then peaceable, gentle, willing to yield, without partiality, and without hypocrisy (James 3: 13-17 NKJV)

Read this passage again and ask yourself questions about yourself and those you associate with. If you are sincere, you may have some things to really pray about.

- **Must be someone who keeps secrets**. Every elder worthy of this office must learn to keep confidential matters confidential. He must be trusted not to betray the trust of other key Christian leaders, Presidents of nations, Governors, men and women in very high positions with sensitive information as their counsel is sought regularly on such matters. If he is self-seeking, he will move around town bragging about his "special connections", telling all who care to listen about who he has been with and where he has been to. This can be very dangerous.

- **Must have a sound marriage, good family life with godly children and well-trained, disciplined, polite disciples** (Titus 1: 5 – 6). To be sure of them you could pay impromptu visits to their offices and watch those around them to see the type of spirit they have.

- **Must not be materialistic and greedy for money, wealth or recognition.** Men like these are very vulnerable. They can do anything in the name of the Lord to achieve their ambitions. They will betray trust, lie, slander, flatter and deceive. More often than not, they render dishonest eye service to impress, are destructive and superficially committed to a cause to achieve their hidden motive. They look for the right opportunity to grab and reveal their real identities. In 1 Peter 5: 1-2, every elder is warned against this evil attitude. Paul when writing to Titus unveiled these deceitful men even further:

> *They profess to know God, but in works they deny Him, being abominable,*

*disobedient, and disqualified for every good work". (*Titus 1:16).

Do not assign important responsibilities to such people. The bible says they are **disqualified.** Therefore, look for mature, established people, who are content with what God has made them. Humility is a sign of true maturity. Some people brag and talk a lot about their humility. Those who are humble do not talk about it. They show it by the way they talk about themselves and their achievements and the way they relate to others. They show it by the way they treat others. And when they are called to serve, they do it not like self-made achievers, self-confident people with a "master of the show attitude", but with meekness. This word humility is still in the bible, so let us grab it and add it to our lives.

As each one has received gifts, minister it to one another, as good stewards of the manifold grace of God. If anyone (this means those at the top-most hierarchy and those who are at the bottom of it, whatever this means) speaks, let him speak as the oracle (one transmitting God's accurate undiluted message) of God. If anyone ministers (serves, occupies an office, leads, etc) let him do it with the ability which God supplies (not with human wisdom and gimmicks) that in all things God may be glorified through Jesus Christ to whom belong the glory (which must not be tampered with) and the dominion forever and ever. Amen (1 Peter 4:10 – 11).

- **Must be reliable and trustworthy.** Their word must be their bond. They must be able to stand by what they say, live and die for it, spend and be spent for the gospel, now and in the future. When an Elder's Forum is this strong, they can give a strong leadership to the people. None of them denies others because of human pressure, no matter where it comes from. None of them identifies with the wicked in order to be in someone's good book. They are principled. Their desired task is honored above tribal and ethnic ties. They have the backbone to set and maintain high standards. Children with money will not be able to buy any of them over. They will not use issues discussed at meetings to curry cheap favors from certain quarters. When working on collective matters, their suggestions will not be motivated by selfish ambition. Above all, they must be strong in prayer and knowledgeable about how these things are done.

- **Must be knowledgeable spiritual warriors.** They know how to do spiritual warfare on earth and in the heavenlies against spiritual hosts of wickedness, rulers of darkness and principal deities or demons with enormous controlling powers. They must not be novices in these matters. They must have eyes which search out hidden things that affect the people, alert minds that search out the unknown, and sensitive observant spirits that pick-up constantly what God is saying concerning them and their city, state or nation. These must not be mean-spirited men and women. They must be interested, like Daniel, in reading and finding out the history of their people and the land they occupy. So that they can revisit any old covenant or dealings by the people of the past with one another, to know whether their ancestors pledged allegiance to God or to Satan.

Daniel was clearly an elder cut out of this mold. He carefully read the scriptures, searching the records to know what God's mind was concerning his generation held in captivity.

> *In the first year of Darius the son of Ahasuerus, of the lineage of the Medes, who was made king over the reading of the Chaldeans – in the first year of his reign, I Daniel, understood by the books the*

number of the years specified by the word of the Lord, given through Jeremiah the prophet, that He would accomplish seventy years in the desolation of Jerusalem (Daniel 9: 1-2).

They should have a rich vocabulary of prayer and expressions for effective spiritual warfare to last them through any fight, no matter how long it takes. They should teach the younger people warfare. They must be very prayerful, experienced and strong in spiritual warfare. Their assignments will include destroying ancient demonic altars, shrines, tokens, trees, evil forests, and evil foundations, unholy covenants, cleansing and making atonement for the land and the people therein.

- **Appreciative of what is good.** Some are angered by other people's successes because they believe they should be the only cock that crows in the city. If they do not preach, who else should? If they do not talk or pray, who else should do so? Such people believe that they have to push down or pull-down others in order to be noticed. They do it with fiery satanic anointing and zeal. Not so for God's elders. They know that everyone is a gift to them and stand to encourage and appreciate good work by others even when they are not involved, consulted or worshipped. This way other people who are successful in their own different callings will feel secure to relate to them.

- **They must be masters of the word of God.** If this word is going to be the parameter by which every issue will be weighed and measured, certified or condemned, then they must know it so well that you cannot toss them around, confuse or manipulate them using the word. Jesus answered and said unto them, ye do err, not knowing the scriptures, nor the power of God." (Matthew 22: 29)

- **They must love God with a burning passion** that they will easily die to defend His kingdom without even thinking about it. They must not love their 'good' reputation; popularity, good position in the city, government or in the church or their salary (stomach) more than doing the will of God. Oh! God give us this type of Godly Elders in Jesus Name!

- **Regular Meetings**
They schedule a time, day and place to meet regularly with God and one another. It is a Covenant Assignment. It is a Kingdom task. Attendance should not be based on circulars and reminders. Everyone called to minister at the *Gate* must be faithful and committed.

During meetings more time should be given to pray and listen to God than discussions.

- **Manning The Observatory**
Different people should be assigned to keep watch over what happens in various sections of the church and society to monitor things for prayers and necessary follow-up actions.

- **They must be willing and Sacrificial**
It is a voluntary task to the Kingdom of our God. Nobody does it to be paid by any man. People who do not understand this will always demand financial gratification for work they do for God. I remember once when one man who joined us to attend meetings and do some occasional work, after a while sent a bill for helping to pray for the city. As unimaginable as this is, it happened. We must come to the understanding that it is a voluntary job done with completely willing and devoted human vessels. It is done for God who has its own adequate way of rewarding His faithful workers when the time comes.

> *Let a man so consider us, as servants of Christ and stewards of the mysteries of God. Moreover, it is required in stewards that one be found faithful. But with me it is a very small thing that I should be judged by you or by a human*

court. In fact, I do not even judge myself. For I know of nothing against myself, yet I am not justified by this; but He who judges me is the Lord. Therefore, judge nothing before the time, until the Lord comes, who will both bring to light the hidden things of darkness and reveal the counsels of the hearts. Then each one's praise will come from God. (1 Corinthians 4: 1–5)

And whatsoever ye do in the word or deed, do all in the name of the Lord Jesus, giving thanks to God and the Father by Him. ...And whatsoever you do, do it heartily, as to the Lord, and not unto men; knowing that of the Lord you shall receive the reward of the inheritance: for you serve the Lord Christ. But he who does wrong will be repaid for what he has done, and there is no partiality. (Colossians 3: 17, 23 – 25).

CHAPTER FIVE

GATES

Webster's Ninth New Collegiate Dictionary defines gates as *"Openings"*. It further explains that a gate is "an *opening* in a wall or fence; a city or castle *entrance* often with defensive structures (as towers): the frame or door that closes a gate; a means of *entrance* or *exit,* etc."

The gates were an important part of any ancient city. They provided the only way of passing through the wall and were normally closed at night and were strengthened by bars of brass or iron. Any important place of public concourse was designated as a gate partly because it was an open space, not usually found elsewhere in a city. Much of the legal business of the city was done there (Ruth 4:11).

The word "gate" is sometimes associated with power, dominion or control. God promised and instructed Abraham, that his posterity would possess the gates of their enemies, their towns, and their fortress, (Genesis 22: 17).

As Abraham's spiritual seed, we must aim to conquer our enemies, and have dominion over them.

The gates of death are the brink or mouth of the grave,

> Psalm 9:13; "……..*You who lift me up from the gates of death.*"

The above definitions are clear and self-explanatory.

When speaking about spiritual gates of significance, we would want to consider personal gates, home/family Gates, compound gates, neighborhood gates, city gates, local government or village gates, state or provincial gates, national gates, continental gates and global and world gates. Each of these gates should serve their purposes or else there will be problems. In Psalm 118:19-21 after God had given David victory he sang:

> *Open to me the gates of righteousness; I will go through them, and I will praise the LORD. This is the gate of the LORD, through which the righteous shall enter. I will praise You, for You have answered me, and have become my salvation.*

In actual fact, gates provide access to places, people cities and situation. Now let us continue to discover, as we look into the word together what the bible says about gates. In the bible a typical gate served the following purposes:

1. A Seat of Power and Authority

In other words, a gate is a place of power and dominion.

That in blessing I will bless thee, and in multiplying I will multiply thy seed as the stars of the heaven, and as the sand which is upon the sea shore, and thy seed shall possess the gate of thy enemies (Genesis 22:17).

The blessings bestowed on Abraham's seed is Divine Power to take over and control every place of power, dominion and decision making of their enemies.

And they blessed Rebecca and said to her: "Our sister, may you become the mother of thousands of ten thousands; And may your descendants possess The gates of those who hate them." (Genesis. 24:60).

Do the wicked have rule over you and the church in your land?

These powerful passages of scripture simply indicate that the children of the righteous who exercise their Authority as legislators at the gates will have dominion over those who hate them. That is a good blessing! By this blessing the scriptures have sentenced everyone who will not like what God will be doing in the lives of the righteous seeds to remain perpetually under their control. Good blessing! Since they would not like your face, let them remain at your back!

2. A Place to Administer Justice

Matters and cases are resolved at the Gate where the Elders sit to administer justice. It is not a place for boys and new comers, no matter how materially successful these may be, it is a place where discipline is enforced and the oppressed released.

> *If a man has a stubborn and rebellious son, who will not obey the voice of his father, or the voice of his mother, and that, when they have chastened him, will not hearken unto them, then shall his father and his mother lay hold on him, and bring him out unto the elders of his city, and unto the gate of his place (Deuteronomy 21:18-19).*

Gates here refer to a place where the wicked and evil men, who take bribes and deny the people justice are brought to the Court of Justice. In this place, we need to pray for righteous Judges to emerge.

(a). Tough cases were settled at the gate. Whatever judgments were given were final, whether spiritually or physically. Immoral fellows who could not exercise self-control sexually were sentenced to death at the gate (Deuteronomy 22: 23-27). In this present loose and immoral generation, the Elders have lots of work to do before God.

(b). **Marital Matters**

Judicial matters over marriage contracts were sorted out and concluded at the Gates. Boaz and Ruth are clear examples Ruth 4:1. So we understand that gates were not just doors or entrances or exits, the gathering of Elders at sensitive entry and meeting locations were called gates.

Have you read Job's role at the Gate? It is powerful. Without any attempts at self-promotion or unnecessary embellishment, the man Job, paints his profile graphically as an Elder at the Gate. Hear him:

When I went out to the gate by the city, when I took my seat in the open square, the young men saw me and hid, and the aged arose and stood; the princes refrained from talking and put their hand on their mouth; the voice of nobles was hushed, and their tongue stuck to the roof of their mouth. When the ear heard, then it blessed me, And when the eye saw, then it approved me; Because I delivered the poor who cried out,

The fatherless and the one who had no helper. The blessing of a perishing man came upon me, and I caused the widow's heart to sing for joy. I put on righteousness, and it clothed me; my justice was like a robe and a turban. I was eyes to the blind, and I was feet to the lame.

I was a father to the poor, and I searched out the case that I did not know. I broke the fangs of the wicked and plucked the victim from his teeth. Men listened to me and waited and kept silence for my counsel. After my words they did not speak again, and my speech settled on them as dew. They waited for me as for the rain, I chose the way for them, and sat as chief; So I dwelt as a king in the army, as one who comforts mourners. (Job 29: 7-17, 21-23, 25).

What have you read? This is honor at its peak. Oh for Elders like this in every city in the world! We would have heaven here on earth.

Amos prophesied against the children of Israel when they resisted righteous men who manned their gates (Amos 5:10, 12, 15).

They hate the one who rebukes in the gate, and they abhor the one who speaks uprightly ...For I know your manifold transgressions and your mighty sins:

> *Afflicting the just and taking bribes; diverting the poor from justice at the gate. Hate evil, love good; Establish justice in the gate. It may be that the LORD God of hosts will be gracious to the remnant of Joseph.*

I know a man who has been there. For being upright and standing up against evil, a wayward generation took up an extensive campaign of defamation against the innocent. But the inevitable result is always Divine Judgment.

3. Sensitive Security Spots

Solomon was instructed by David to appoint men to guard the gates and he did (2 Chronicles 8:14).

> *And, according to the order of David his father, he appointed the divisions of the priests for their service, the Levites for their duties (to praise and serve before the priests) as the duty of each day required, and the gatekeepers by their divisions at each gate; for so David the man of God had commanded.*

4. A Control Point

Nehemiah used the gates to stop merchandising in Israel on the Sabbath. He restricted the entrance of non-Jews who had no respect for the Sabbath, who brought in their wares to sell when people should be worshipping God (Nehemiah 13:14-22).

In the same vein, where there are watchful Elders at the city gates, they will notice when new ungodly trends, trades, (like those by the witch doctors) polluting movies and such are brought into the city or shown on their television stations or radio stations or even in the local churches in the city.

We read in Esther Chapters 4 & 6 when Mordecai served at the King's gate, it was not as a minor security detail, but as someone who had control of the security of the Government or Royal House. It was not a minor place to serve.

> *When Mordecai learned all that had happened, he tore his clothes and put on sackcloth and ashes and went out into the midst of the city. He cried out with a loud and bitter cry. He went as far as the front of the king's gate, for no one might enter the king's gate clothed with sackcloth. (Esther 4: 1-2)*

> *Then the king said to Haman, "Hurry, take the robe and the horse, as you have suggested, and do so for Mordecai the Jew who sits within the king's gate! Leave nothing undone of all that you have spoken." So Haman took the robe and the horse, arrayed Mordecai and led him on horseback through the city square,*

and proclaimed before him. "Thus shall it be done to the man whom the king delights to honor!" Afterward Mordecai went back to the king's gate. But Haman hurried to his house, mourning and with his head covered. (Esther 6: 10-12).

It was at this gate that Mordecai discovered a plot to assassinate the King and saved his life. Here evil plans (Satanic and human) can be discovered, intercepted and destroyed to save your family, city, the people and the government of the day. Even so today, if you have a strong gate, your goods are better secured.

5. A Godly Monitoring Caucus

Elders should first feel the burden of the land at the gate and respond accordingly

Wail, O gate! Cry, O city! All you of Philistia are dissolved; For smoke will come from the north, and no one will be alone in his appointed times. (Isaiah 14:31).

When Isaiah heard a terrible prophecy against the Philistines who celebrated at the death of King Ahaz of Judah, he sent it first to the men at their gates! But they failed to do something to avert the danger, probably because there were no godly elders, or knowledgeable ones, who knew how to respond to such things. Read what happened when the prophecy was fulfilled in 2 Kings 18.

> *Now it came to pass in the third year of Hoshea the son of Elah, king of Israel, that Hezekiah the son of Ahaz, king of Judah, began to reign. He subdued the Philistines, as far as Gaza and its territory, from watchtower to fortified city. (who could not do their job – so the destruction started there) to the fenced cit. (2 Kings 18: 1, 8).*

Does your city have Godly, upright and mature Elders at the Gates who are faithful and conscientious about their role in the city? Are they knowledgeable in handling divine messages or do they laugh and make mockery of prophecies? There may not be much hope for cities whose spiritual gates lack knowledgeable Christian Elders. The fetish satanic elders will use the gates to enhance satanic influence in the land. And of course, everyone will suffer the consequences.

6. **The City Gate is a Stronghold of the City.**
    To be smitten at your own gate is to be defeated shamefully. When the enemy brings the battle to your gate, he puts you on the defensive. If you have weak men at the gate, that is the end. You will be a slave – physically

or spiritually to the enemies that defeat you at your gate. They determine when, where and how far you can go. They rule or exercise control over your culture, lifestyle, spiritual, social and economic climate. That is why Isaiah said God likes to give strength to those who take the battle to the gates of their enemies

> **6***And for a spirit of judgment to him that sitteth in judgment, and for strength to them that turn the battle to the gate.* (Isaiah 28:6)

This agrees with Christ's prediction in Matthew 16:18.

> *"... I will build my church (not a split polarized one); and the gates (which suggests they are many) of hell shall not prevail against it".*

This means the battles should actually be fought at the *enemy's* gates. Whoever brings the battles to the gates determines the tempo and style of the fight, because those on the defensive will have to follow after the attacking force. We must be on the offensive, harassing the kingdom of darkness.

Have you ever wondered why Saul was able to succeed in persecuting and intimidating the church in Jerusalem but could not as much as enter into the small city of Damascus? The elders at Damascus policed their spiritual gates. They went to God in prayer, built a spiritual hedge around their city and asked Christ to please man their gate. When Saul hit the hedge, the "Gateman" called out to him demanding, "Saul, Saul why are persecuting me?" While the gates of Jerusalem were open to Saul, the gates of Damascus were not. You can close the gates of your life, family, ministry, city or nation against any invading enemy and they will not enter in Jesus Name!

David in Psalm 127:5 said;

> *"The good children of a strongman would speak with their enemies at the gates"*

The opposite is that the bad children of bad men quarrel in the house. By their striving, the gates are left unmanned. And the people within the city are vulnerable to attack.

7. Gates are Crucial Places

When the heavenly messengers visited Sodom and Gomorrah, they met Lot sitting at the Gate of the city (Genesis 19:1). The purpose of their visit was revealed to the man at the Gate. Even though he was a stranger, he had the honor of receiving such privileged and sensitive information because he was strategically positioned at the Gate. He was the one who knew what to do to stay alive. Pray for sincere, godly, faithful men and women to guard the spiritual gates of your family, compound, neighborhood and city. Whether they are indigenous or non-indigenous people, if God put them there, you better honor and listen to them for your own good. Not everybody can man the gates. Are all who man your physical gates loyal to God? Many Christians consciously employ Muslims to man their physical gates for them and they see nothing wrong with that arrangement. They are mobile altars that are a gateway to satanic spiritual activities. They use your gate as their devilish altar. There is no way it will not affect other things around you if you do not handle it spiritually. Be wise.

When Aaron and the children of Israel built a golden calf to offend the Lord, Moses stood at the Gate to handle the matter (Exodus 32:26).

> *Then Moses stood in the gate of the camp, and said, Who is on the LORD's side? Let him come unto me. And all the sons of Levi gathered themselves together unto him.*

The Levites who responded at the gate earned a special place and blessing from the Lord. When the Elders at the Gate call on you, how do you respond to it? Not every elder can be at the gate. It is a sacrifice. It is hard work. I have been there and I am still there. It limits your personal comfort and movement, because you cannot go too far from your post or else you will give the enemy an open gate to invade the land and cause much harm. You cannot attend to your personal matters as you used to do. So let no man envy and plan to destroy you because like Mordecai, God put you at the Gate in your land or in a foreign land. It is very demanding if you want to do a good and effective job. You have to come before God regularly in fasting, stay spiritually and physically awake to carry out prophetic actions when others are sleeping you are facing the dangers of going to some locations to do warfare. Even the old wise Daniel was a man of the gates.

> *Then Daniel requested of the King, and he set Shadrach, Meshach and Abed- nego, over the affairs of the province of Babylon, but Daniel sat in the gate of the king (Daniel 2:49)*

Wise old men knew where to stay. In my village, we have a family hut usually built at the center of the compound. It is called 'Ovu' in my language. This is where the oldest man of the family likes to stay always. He stays there to monitor who comes in or goes out of the compound. Any straying boy coming to visit his girlfriend without any serious message, on sighting him, quickly makes a U-turn. But a compound without a responsible and feared old man is invaded every now and then by bad boys and other wicked people, because there is no one who can inspire fear in them. What was it that Nehemiah saw that made him lose interest in the beauty and glamour of the royal house? Why did he lose appetite for food and was crying like a baby? "The gates thereof are burned with fire", his informants told him. This caused him much pain and sorrow.

> *So it was, when I heard these words, that I sat down and wept, and mourned for many days; I was fasting and praying before the God of heaven."* Nehemiah 1:4

Several spiritual and physical afflictions, including great distress and reproaches come to people without healthy gates, or people whose gates are, as it were, burnt with fire. What has happened to the gates of the place of your maturity or the city, state or province where you live? How strong and healthy are the spiritual gates of your country? Those who lose do so because the gates are unguarded. Those who ravage your lives and economy do so because your gates are "**burnt with fire**".

While many ate and drank, Nehemiah who knew the security and spiritual implications of having destroyed gates mourned. Do you have knowledge and understanding of this? Then why will your gates remain broken and unguarded? (Lamentations 1: 4).

> *The roads to Zion mourn because no one comes to the set feasts. All her gates are desolate; Her priests sigh, Her virgins are afflicted, And she is in bitterness.*

This is not a political thing but spiritual. But it has a wholesome implication because it affects every aspect of the people's life.

Elders At The Gates

Elders At The Gates

CHAPTER SIX

TYPES OF GATES

I mentioned in the last chapter that there are different types of gates. Here I will briefly outline some.

Personal And Human Gates

There are several gates in the human body; unfortunately, many get into trouble because they do not guard their human gates.

Below are some of the gates within your body and spirit you must guard properly:

A) The eyes

The eyes feed the mind and the brain. The brain interprets whatever the eyes see and suggests immediate line of action. Job made a covenant with his eyes on what to focus on and what not to watch. If God's eyes are too pure to behold iniquity, ours should not watch pornographic pictures, movies, and any such thing meant to feed filthy hearts. Job the righteous man and John the beloved have very sound counsel to offer us in this regard. Job says: *"I have made a covenant with my eyes; Why then should I look upon a young woman? Job 31:1*

In John's first epistle, we read these words:

> *Love not the world, neither the things that are in the world. If any man loves the world, the love of the Father is not in him. For all that is in the world, the lust of the flesh, and the lust of the eyes, and the pride of life, is not of the Father, but is of the world"* (1 John 2:15-16).

Here is a biblical instruction not to feed your eyes with lustful worldly stuff. Any disobedience has an ugly consequence. Your eyes, if not controlled, will let in pollution into your heart and spirit. Anything that your eyes see, is transmitted to several organs in your body within seconds. Jesus himself, teaching on the subject of the eye made the following statement.

> *The lamp of the body is the eye. If therefore your eye is good, your whole body will be full of light. But if your eye is bad, your whole body will be full of darkness. If therefore the light that is in you is darkness, how great is that darkness! Matthew 6:22-23*

This passage reporting a teaching by Christ makes it very clear why you have to be careful what your eyes watch. In Luke 11:35 Jesus said:

"Take heed therefore, (this means be very careful), that the light which is in thee be not darkness".

B) The Mouth

This is another human gate. What enters through this gate matters as much as what goes out. If you let in good food into your body, it will be nourished, but if you eat or drink poison, death could result. The mouth is neither for cigarettes, nor intoxicating drinks. It is for eating or drinking healthy food or drinks.

It can utter life-giving words and at the same time destroy individuals, families, communities and even nations. So, it should be guarded. James calls the tongue a world of iniquity!

> *For we all stumble in many things. If anyone does not stumble in word, he is a perfect man, able also to bridle the whole body. And the tongue is a fire, a world of iniquity. The tongue is so set among our members that it defiles the whole body, and sets on fire the course of nature; and it is set on fire by hell (James 3:2, 6)*

Many sweet relationships and great associations have been irreversibly destroyed by allowing destructive things to flow through this gate. This shows you how delicate this gate is. You have to watch over it, guard it carefully and intelligently, so that you do not burn down your world. Think of it. The bible says you are ensnared by the words of your mouth. This means you can live a snare free life if you learn how to bridle this gate. Solomon said even a fool, when he controls this gate is termed wise. So you can be wise by guarding this gate.

C) The ear

The ear is another important gate. You can grow or be destroyed by what enters through this gate. The scripture says,

> *"Faith comes by hearing and hearing the word of God"* (Romans 10: 17).

On the other hand, fear comes by hearing, and hearing the word of the devil, through people or your mind. If your faith is the victory that overcomes the world and you deflate it by listening to faith killing counsels, you are gone. So watch that ear gate.

D) The umbilical cord

This is the supply route of food and nourishment from a pregnant mother to the baby. Other spiritual things pass through the same gate unto the baby. Most times physical and spiritual traits existing in the mother are transferred to the un-born baby through the umbilical gate. When dealing with personal deliverance, you will learn more about this. This is a gate that needs to be addressed as soon as the baby is born. And please do not take your umbilical cord to your village to give to your ancestors. You are not an apron string to be tied to anybody. You are a miracle on your own, released from heaven and sent to earth on a mission. Do not tie yourself to the success or failure of your ancestors. Prayerfully dispose of your umbilical cord or that of your children. Commit such to the hands of the Lord. That is a service gate. Ezekiel 16:1-4. Since this is not the main subject of this book, we cannot go further than this.

E) Sexual organs

The sexual organs of both sexes are gates into our bodies and our spirits. Diseases and demons are easily transmitted and transferred both ways. Condoms do not hold evil spirits back! Covenants are also easily cut through these gates. Guard them jealously. Do not throw this gate open to your own ruin.

F) Hands

The bible speaks very much about clean hands and pure hearts. The works of our hands bring to us blessings or curses.

Healing flows through our hands. When our spirit is defiled, spiritual pollution can be transferred to the heads of innocent people. Power can be transferred through your palms.

Some years ago, I just finished ministering at St. Peters Anglican Church, Rumuepirikon in Port Harcourt where I live and was tired. But a lady came to me in desperation saying her relation was about to die in the hospital. Medication was not helping the matter. She demanded I go back to the hospital with her to pray for the relation so he would not die. I wanted to help but my physical body was tired. I asked her to stretch forth her two hands and place them on mine. I spoke a few words in the Name of Jesus Christ and asked her to go and lay those hands upon the dying fellow in the hospital. By faith I let her know that even if the person was dead, he would rise. She went to the hospital, did exactly that, and the sick recovered. Power flowed through my hands into her hands. The hands are gates! Habakkuk saw a revelation on this.

God came from Teman, the Holy One from Mount Paran. His glory covered the heavens, and the earth was full of His praise. His brightness was like the light; He had rays flashing from His hand, and there His power was hidden (Habakkuk 3:3-4).

G) The head

You need not be told that by laying hands on your head, you can be filled with the Holy Spirit as well as be filled with something else. Physically, even heat evaporates more through the head than the skin. That is why we cover our head to be warm. The head is also a human gate. The bible encourages us that our head should not lack God's oil.

Let thy garments be always white; and let thy head lack no ointment" (Ecclesiastes 9:8).

Maintain and service this gate regularly. Samson thought the oil of anointing was still there and would be kept safe if he went out to do what he did before, but he never returned, because he did not guard the anointing. Guard this gate; it is called the head gate. What happens there has enormous consequences.

The Place Of Your Nativity

During a gubernatorial election in one of the states in the Federation of Nigeria, part of the steps the Holy Spirit led the intercessors to take was to go to the town of nativity of a particular candidate whom Christians were backing to deliver him because his opponents had tried to undo him through that gate.

> *30 Shall I cause it to return into his sheath? I will judge thee in the place where thou wast created, in the land of thy nativity. Ezekiel 21:30*

H) Family Gates

These are openings through which the enemy can invade a home or family or cast away your goods spiritually or physically. They include your house doors, windows, physical gates and any one whom you authorize to speak into your lives as a married couple. He may be a pastor, counselor or prayer partner. Others include parents or parents in-law, friends or people whom you listen to. These doors include your staff and housemaids and cooks who prepare what you eat and drink. Your gynecologist has a great access into your life and family and has great spiritual access not only to the woman, but also through her to the husband and to the children delivered by him or her. So you need to watch these areas prayerfully.

I had a tough time ministering deliverance to a boy at Ejigbo in Lagos, who, either the gynecologist or the midwife at the hospital, used the placenta after he was born, to initiate him into a covenant into two terrible cults with marine powers. As he grew up, the suffering of the family increased, speedily leading to a downward spiral. They ate with the boy, slept in the same house with him, went to church with him and even prayed regularly with him but he was an advanced wizard, older in the evil world than he was physically. He made mockery of religious prayers and anointing oil. It is a long story.

Be watchful over who handles your wife in the hospital. What about the gateman at your gate, your drivers and artisan workers? Many masters have been killed because of the information their gatekeepers gave out to the wrong people. They overhear sensitive discussions and go out to share them with evil men. Incidentally, these gatekeepers or night guards often know the robbers because they meet them in the night. A gang of armed robbers that were caught somewhere in Nigeria revealed that their leader was a *"maiguard"* – a night guard selling provisions in a small hut somewhere. Who guards your family gates? In the villages, the front door is a gate. The wicked come there to drop their fetish objects. Sometimes they do it at the center or one side of the entrance to the compound, that is a gate.

I) Neighborhood/Estate Gates

Neighborhood or Estate Gates exist. Of course, you know that in some neighborhoods you cannot enter without going through a gate. The same way there are physical gates into the neighborhood, that is how you also have spiritual gates.

J) City Gates

Cities have gates. These are entry points into the city. It could be a waterfront, or a bridge across a river or an entrance by a simple flat surface road, seaport or airport. If you wake up and visit these locations between 12 midnight and 2.00 a.m., you will be surprised to find out the number of people who worship Satan, who do not sleep while others sleep, but go to the gates to seek for power from Satan. At those nocturnal meetings, they actively raise and service evil altars for one diabolical reason or the other. This happens in every part of the world.

There is no part of the universe where the devil does not have agents. If the city has faithful godly elders that watch over the gates, the spirit of the Lord will constantly use them to continue to undo the works of darkness and release life, peace and prosperity to the city. Where you see high divorce rates, broken homes and marriages, high crime rates, prostitution, contention among church leaders, drunkenness, these are signs of high-level demonic activities in that city.

K) State/Province Gates

States or provinces have gates. The major entrance through which one crosses from one sovereign state to another is a gateway. Here, important national and international guests are handed over from one governor to the other. Powerful actions and activities that influence an entire state take place in those places. With prophetic actions, a state can be sealed or opened up at her gates. Any of these actions by Christians must be inspired and directed by the Holy Spirit.

One day the Lord told us to gather at midnight for battle. On arrival, he sent us to the gates of our own city. We were shocked to meet a big crowd of believers of a popular false religion in my country making sacrifices by a riverbank at midnight. They erected an altar to hinder a particular candidate of a political party from winning an election in that state. Because the Lord through the available, effective and loyal elders did a series of spiritual warfare against the high level sorcery, the candidate who believed in these fetish powers lost in the election. Unfortunately, there were states where there were no Christian elders at the gates and the Christian candidates lost despite very clear signs that he was likely to win. Power is given and taken at the gates. Even when God has given you a place, you may still have to contend with the opposing powers of darkness to physically possess it.

> *Rise take your journey, and cross over the River Arnon. Look, I have given into your hand Sihon the Amorite, king of Heshbon, and his land. Begin to possess it and engage him in battle (Deuteronomy 2:24).*

An abuse of the grace doctrine can be just as harmful as the ignorance that led many African Christians to an early death. Many of these good men went to an early grave by the presumptuous refusal of medical attention in the name of "Faith". Active elders at the gate can control virtually everything that happens in their city on their knees. They must always have among them at prayer times, people who flow in the important governmental graces like the Apostolic, the Evangelistic, the Prophetic, the Teacher, the Pastor, Administrators, Helps, Mercy, etc. They need a rich spiritual house, rich in giftings and graces. This facilitates their work. When the ear hears well and the eyes see well, the brain can go to work, so that other parts of the body will act accordingly. If the eyes and the ears are not available, the brain will have limited information and will function with difficulty. The entire body would run the risk of not being able to move at all.

L) National Gates

National gates exist. They include all key positions and offices of influence in the nations such as:

a. The office of the President of the nation, and other very sensitive executive offices like that of the Governor or the mayor

b. The Courts of Justice

c. The Judiciary

d. The Central Bank and Ministry of finance controlling and influencing the Economic Gate.

e. The Spiritual Gates - Churches, mosques, occult altars, fetish altars and the like.

f. The Media Gate like the TV houses, Cable TV networks, Radio Stations, Newspapers, bloggers and the like.

g. The Entertainment Gate through which all sorts of wickedness is introduced in the form of carnivals, masquerades, dance types, etc.

h. Education Gate controlled by those who prepare the curriculum and choose the text books for the first and secondary levels of education.

i. Physical Gates which will include International Airports, Sea Ports, major land gateways into the nation.

j. Places of interest where public altars exist like the independence square in Nigeria where the altar of the country's existence is located, the sea and airports and their connecting roads with other nations. It is impossible for foreigners to legally enter into other countries without going through immigration services. They are the government Gatekeepers. There are also the equivalent of these in the spirit realms.

More information of Spiritual Gates

There are Global Gates. Have you ever wondered why the prophets of Israel chose to locate their schools of the prophets in places like Gilgal where Elijah lived? Or in other places such as Bethel and Jordan? At Gilgal, Joshua circumcised the men who made up the troops in God's replacement Army led by the "Captain of God's Hosts" to take Israel into the Promised Land. It was there the reproach of Egypt, which had followed them for forty-one and half years, was removed. It was there the heavens opened and the Captain of the Lord's Army came to take command because there was a new, unpolluted Army he could work with. It was there Israel celebrated Passover, an annual event they did not celebrate for decades due to rebellious living. It was at Gilgal where manna and quail; the temporary non-lasting blessings ceased and gave way to permanent blessings – assorted fruits of the land, which they could store. Gilgal was a gateway to heaven.

Bethel, of course you know the story. By the reason of multiple altars raised at Bethel unto the Lord, His presence was so strong there that the heavens were open above it.

> *Then he dreamed, and behold, a ladder was set up on the earth, and its top reached to heaven; and there the angels*

> *of God were ascending and descending on it. And behold, the LORD stood above it and said: "I am the LORD God of Abraham your father and the God of Isaac; the land on which you lie I will give to you and your descendants......Then Jacob awoke from his sleep and said, "Surely the LORD is in this place, and I did not know it." (Genesis 28:12-13,16).*

Other things recorded in the scriptures happened to make the Prophets settle down in Bethel, which means "the house of God." Who would not like to dwell there? It was a spiritual gateway to heaven. Now, the other side of the story: if the Godly Altars set up by Abraham and Isaac opened the heavens to that location, evil altars set up by the agents of Satan also have the power to open gate ways to hell. They exist by roadsides, waterfronts, by shrines, forests, etc. So, the elders in the land must identify these gateways to hell and shut them to reduce the traffic of evil spirits and activities in their city. And finally, another gateway to heaven that attracted old prophets was Jordan. God would not let Israel cross the Jordan without fresh a consecration.

> *And Joshua said to the people sanctify yourselves, for tomorrow the Lord will do wonders among you". And the Lord said to*

Joshua, "This day will I begin to magnify you in the sight of all Israel, that they may know that as I was with Moses, so I will be with you (Joshua 3:5, 7).

Most times people come to God for the miracles and wonders but do not want to sanctify themselves or live sanctified lives to keep His presence. Please do not ask anyone to pray for God to do a miracle for you if you have not decided finally to do away with every filthiness. Living a holy and sanctified life facilitates the flow of the miraculous. Joshua's magnifying experiences were reserved for him at Jordan. The seventh verse of Joshua chapter three reminds me of the later incidence between Elijah and Elisha. It was when Elisha crossed the Jordan that Elijah asked him what he wanted. His double portion anointing was to be given after crossing this same river Jordan.

Spiritually, it takes only those who consecrate and dedicate their lives totally to God's agenda to cross the Jordan. And having spiritual insight helps those with higher spiritual mantles to see and act appropriately. It is like your ministry going International. It is a great promotion. Jordan in those days was one place that when you crossed it or went through it, you broke open the limitations of your ministry. You remember it was at Jordan where Jesus got baptized. It was there the heaven opened and God spoke in an audible voice, which others could hear, introducing Christ to the world. It was there also that the Holy Spirit descended upon Him like a physical dove and men's eyes saw it. Jordan must have been a wonderful place! It was only after this incident that the Holy Spirit led Jesus into the wilderness to fast and commence his confrontation with Satan and the kingdom of darkness just before He made His ministry public. He had to go through Jordan to fulfill all righteousness and pick up what He needed to go public. The heavenly chariots and their riders accessed the earth to pick up Elijah through the Jordan gate. So Jordan had a major spiritual gate that would allow heavenly spiritual beings and chariots to come down and be seen with physical eyes. While Moses could strike the Red Sea and create a road that had not existed here on the physical plane before, he was forbidden from striking Jordan. The Ark physically representing the Presence of God had to go before the Israelites as they crossed the Jordan.

Spiritually blind Naaman, the captain of the Syrian army, ignorantly began to compare the powerless Abanah and Pharfar rivers of Damascus with the River Jordan. Elisha knew very well how strong the Presence of God was over the Jordan, he did not waste his time praying or arguing with Namaan. Maybe the spiritual foundation and health of Naaman needed something more dramatic than words of prayer. Naaman means pleasant, but his life was a mixture of the sweet and the bitter. Elisha knew Jordan would do it and instructed him to go there and ensured perfect submission to the abiding Presence of God at that gate. Naaman had to dip himself in the water, invariably bowing to God each time he dipped himself for seven good times. This symbolized or spoke of perfection and God's Divine Will and timing. Who says God does not have a great sense of humor? Elisha did not want to touch that glory, so he refused to show up at all. He was also not interested in the gifts Naaman brought for him. Many today would have come out and taken photographs with the big officer for further publicity and promotion. Jordan is a powerful Global Gate.

L) Global Gates

Global Gates are divided into two. Firstly, the human gates and secondly, the political gates. Such men who are Presidents of the G8 nations are global human gates.

Political Gates include institutions such as United Nations (UN) and their ancillary bodies, major cable TV Stations like CNN or BBC are global gates.

Major airports like London Heathrow or New York JFK Airport are further examples of global gates.

M) Continental Gates

Such continental bodies like European Union, African Union and the like are continental gates.

Maintain the Gates

Gates can be closed. We all know that. When an altar is destroyed or not serviced for a great length of time, the gate could be closed. This does not mean that when the right things are done that they cannot be reopened. Every generation should pray to God to raise for them Elders like Joshua, Elijah, Elisha, John the Baptist and others, who know and understand how to identify gates, what to do with them and how to use them as God has divinely designed.

Elders At The Gates

CHAPTER SEVEN

BATTLES AT THE GATES

In the year 2012, a Mayor of one of the outstanding cities in the State of Florida in USA requested for me to be his mentor and spiritual cover. I asked him why me since I am not a politician and do not reside in USA, he said to me, "the seat of Government is the seat of every evil". He went further to say that "the battle between good and evil is very fierce there." Satan has always been interested in the seat or gate of power from the beginning. Let us take a look at Isaiah 14:12-15;

> *How you are fallen from heaven, O Lucifer, son of the morning! How you are cut down to the ground, you who weakened the nations! For you have said in your heart: 'I will ascend into heaven, I will exalt my throne above the stars of God; I will also sit on the mount of the congregation On the farthest sides of the north; I will ascend above the heights of the clouds, I will be like the Most High. 'Yet you shall be brought down to Sheol, To the lowest depths of the Pit.*

See the blessings of God over Abraham in Genesis 22:16-17 which reads:

> "...*By Myself I have sworn, says the LORD, because you have done this thing, and have not withheld your son, your only son -"blessing I will bless you, and multiplying I will multiply your descendants as the stars of the heaven and as the sand which is on the seashore; and your descendants shall* **possess the gate of their enemies***"*

See also the blessings of the family of Rebekah over her and the future sons of Jacob in Genesis 24:60, which reads;

> *And they blessed Rebekah and said to her: "Our sister, may you become The mother of thousands of ten thousands; And may your descendants possess the gates of those who hate them.*

To *"possess the gates of your enemies"* means that you will **overpower** your enemies, **exercise dominion** and **control** over them. This blessing is actualized only through warfare at the gates.

This reminds me of what God said to Moses in Deuteronomy 2:24-25.

> *Rise, take your journey, and cross over the River Arnon. Look, I have given into your*

hand Sihon the Amorite, **king of Heshbon** *(the gate of Political power), and his land. Begin to possess it and engage him in battle. 'This day I will begin to put the dread and fear of you upon the nations under the whole heaven, who shall hear the report of you, and shall tremble and be in anguish because of you.*

In Isaiah 28:5-6, we read:

In that day the LORD of hosts will be For a crown of glory and a diadem of beauty To the remnant of His people, For a spirit of justice to him who sits in judgment, And for strength to those who turn back the battle at the gate.

Now let me put down a list of sectors of our national and community life that are gates, which means places of control, dominion and power:

Political Gate
Economic Gate
Media Gate
Education Gate
Security Gate
Spiritual Gate
Entertainment Gate

Political Gate

Daniel, the chief of the wise men in Babylon once said to King Nebuchadnezzar, *"set Shadrach, Meshach, and Abed-Nego over the affairs of the province of Babylon; but **Daniel sat in the gate** of the King* (Daniel 2:49).

The chief of the wise men certainly would know more than the average man or even other wise men. He knew he could coordinate the present welfare and the future well-being of his people, the Jews, from the King's gate more easily.

Nations, states and cities rise and fall according to the leadership abilities of their Heads of States, Governors or Mayors, who occupy the Government Gate. This Gate controls the Administration of Justice and legislates what becomes rules and laws governing the people, controlling immigration, security forces and determines how these operate. It influences what happens in all the other Gates.

That's why King David wrote:

> *"when the righteous rules (controls the political gate), the people rejoice, but when the wicked rules, the people mourn"* (Proverbs 29:2)

"The King (or Head of State) establishes the land by justice, but he who receives it overthrows it" (Proverbs 29:4).

Whether his wife receives on his or her behalf or his aids, the consequence is the same. It means the rise and fall of a nation is determined by the character, morality and practical value system of whoever occupies the political gate as well as his or her spouse.

Economic Gate

Poor economies cannot do much. On the other hand, economic world powers seem to have their way. Those who occupy this gate have great control of what happens in their environment. They "pay the piper and so dictate the tune." The Bible recognizes the strong influence of this gate when the author of Ecclesiastes says in Ecclesiastes 10:19b:

"... money answers everything"

In the world we live in today, if you have the money, you can purchase almost anything your heart desires.

Media Gate

The media gate is very powerful. Public opinion is swayed in different directions by the media.

Evil can be promoted, legalized and effectively sold to the innocent populace by the use of the media. The righteous could be made to look sinful and the wicked and fraudulent made a hero by the use of the media. Through the print-media, web-media, radio and television, a society of people could be positively transformed or destroyed, drawn to God or to anything but God. This is why those who control the political gate fight to control this gate as well.

Education Gate

This gate is a strong gate of wisdom, knowledge, culture, empowerment and disempowerment. The future and the present of the people are molded at this gate.

History is created, preserved and distorted at this gate. The training, mental empowerment, philosophies of life, value systems, beliefs, official language, customs and traditions of a people can be destroyed easily over time at this gate. Therefore, those who control this gate can determine the future of the people involved. The people can be limited by giving them limited education. On the other hand, they can be made great by providing them with a broad based relevant, quality high education. The knowledge of God or Satan, good and evil can be taught here as a bedrock for every other thing.

Security

The Military, Air Force, Navy, Police and Civil Defense Corps are all security arms of the Government. They take charge of the physical, land, water and air gates. Their leaders in themselves are gates that exercise control, dominion, and authority wherever they are deployed. They can be used by the wicked to stop the righteous from doing what things they want to do. Over the centuries, we have seen all sorts of abuses by those who occupy this gate.

Spiritual Gate

This is the oldest gate. God, the origin of all gates is a Gate, and a Gate-Keeper. Jesus said,

> ***I am the door***. *If anyone enters by me, he will be saved, and will go in and out and find pasture*" (John 10:9)
>
> "*Most assuredly, I say to you, **I am the door** of the sheep*" (John 10:7)

The Almighty God opens and locks any and every gate.

> *Thus says the LORD to His anointed, To Cyrus, whose right hand I have held to subdue nations before him And loose the armor of kings, To open before him the double doors, So that the gates will not be shut. I will go before you And make the*

> *crooked places straight; I will break in pieces the gates of bronze And cut the bars of iron. I will give you the treasures of darkness And hidden riches of secret places, That you may know that I, the LORD, Who call you by your name, Am the God of Israel* (Isaiah 45:1-3)

In Revelation 3:7, Jesus said;

> *And to the angel of the church in Philadelphia write, 'These things says He who is holy, He who is true, He who has the key of David, He who opens, and no one shuts, and shuts and no one opens'.*

He is the one who gives gate keepers powers and influences at the gates

> *In that day the LORD of hosts will be for a crown of glory and a diadem of beauty To the remnant of His people, For a spirit of justice to him who sits in judgment, And for strength to those who turn back the battle at the gate-(*Isaiah 28:5, 6)

Everyone must reckon with God because all authentic power flows from Him. King David wrote in Psalms 62:11:

> *"God has spoken once, twice I have heard this: That power belongs to God."*

A lot of negotiations go on at this gate. All those who have ever had true and lasting success were positively connected to this gate. This gate is strengthened by the establishment of either good or evil altars.

Satan uses the spirit realm as well. He is a spirit and the father of all spiritual wickedness. He uses such spiritual gates as the occultic altars, evil shrines, voodoo and witchcraft altars to empower himself and his cohorts. The altars provide legal authority for Satan to function (Judges 6:25-27).

The Mystery of Altars

An altar is a place consecrated to offer sacrifices to God. It is a meeting place between God and man. Noah, Abraham, Gideon, Jacob and many others met with God and entered into major covenants with God at different altars.

In Genesis 28:10-19, we read that Jacob slept on a location where his father had raised an altar in the past and had an awesome experience.

First, he had an informative dream in the night during which time his spiritual eyes were opened. He saw a ladder on earth whose top reached the heavens. Angels descended from and ascended to heaven on that ladder ministering to the location. He exclaimed, "Wow! This must be the house of God, a spiritual gateway and God must be residing here!" He quickly woke up and worshipped God, made vows to the Lord and offered a sacrifice of oil on the altar he subsequently raised.

Altars are spiritual gateways for regular angelic or demonic trafficking. It is a resting place of spirits. It's a meeting place between man and spirits. It is the place of exchange; man brings his sacrifices to the altar and receives what he needs from the spirit world. It is a place where men enter into Covenants with God. The worshippers of Satan do the same.

Altars are in sizes, namely: personal, family, city, national, continental and global altars. Their strength differs according to their sizes.

Raising an altar on a location in a community changes the spiritual ownership of that community and what happens from that moment onwards (Judges 6:25-27). It declares on whose side the community belongs, either God, Baal or Satan. A good knowledge of the mysteries of altars will equip a spiritual warrior to overturn the gains of the enemy much easily for a very long time and partner with the Most High God to do remarkable exploits.

Entertainment Gate

Children and adults alike love entertainment - whatever makes them laugh, happy, excited and get relieved from stress.

The enemy subtly packages his ideologies and concepts into these areas. Through films children and youth have learnt such vices as violence, stealing, armed robbery, kidnapping, witchcraft and satanic worship. Through novels like Harry Potter, children and the parents have become possessed by witchcraft spirits.

From going to movies, children and youths have become promiscuous, drunkards and drug addicts. The entertainment gate has ruined many. Young people have died in the thousands because of drinking and driving.

Summary

Battles at the gates are fought by mature men and women who occupy top leadership positions at these gates - spiritual, political, economic, education, media, and security/defense gates. When younger ones get involved, they must do so with the covering and supervision of experienced powerful mature leaders.

The wicked approach warfare at the gates with everything accessible to them: money, political connections, satanic forces, threats to life and family, everything at their disposal.

The righteous must not leave any stone unturned but must also fight to take charge of these gates with the combination of powerful Apostolic and Prophetic prayers, fasting, careful planning and execution, mobilized group intercession, prophetic actions, sacrificial spending, networking and unshakeable faith in God.

Those who control these gates determine the fate of others. If anyone should be in charge of them, it must be Christians. It is written "we can do all things through Christ who strengthens us."(Philippians 4:13).

If you are a Christian who by divine design finds yourself at any of these gates, fight to take full control of it and raise an army of godly men and women to strengthen your control at your gate. Those who control these gates rule their world.

Elders At The Gates

CHAPTER EIGHT

HOW TO BRING HEALING TO THE LAND

Many of us Christians are going through all sorts of struggles because of bad spiritual, marital, academic, social, and economic foundations so are our family members and cities.

Some have practiced idolatry and some from idolatrous family backgrounds. Some have been involved in occultic practices, palm reading, horoscope, et cetera, attracting inevitable evil consequences. Some have shed blood by abortion, sacrifices or violence. Some by deceit, cheating and immoral living have attracted curses and spiritual death to their lives and families.

Some locations, neighborhoods, cities, countries or local government areas, governments of rural communities and nations have attracted curses, judgment and death to themselves by acts of wickedness and sin.

If you have sensitive Elders at the Gates such that Jericho had in their time, they must do something to bring healing to the land. If you are truly serious and desirous of personal freedom like

Apostle Paul, you must be willing to obey God totally and be free.

I have seen, heard and read about great and celebrated names who are slaves to immoral living and disgusting secret sins, whose personal secret struggles with unstable marriage is embarrassing to say the least.

Personal Deliverance

As a person, seek for help quickly. St Paul did exactly that.

> *I do not understand what I do. For what I want to do I do not do, but what I hate I do.....O wretched man that I am! Who will deliver me from this body of death? 25 I thank God — through Jesus Christ our Lord! So then, with the mind I myself serve the law of God, but with the flesh the law of sin." (Romans 7:15, 24)*

> *Our fathers sinned and are no more, but we bear their Iniquities. (Lamentation 5:7)*

You may have need to take the steps I am going to mention later. Where you do not experience total freedom and liberty, meet and receive ministry from someone who knows, understands and has the grace to minister powerfully personal deliverance to the saints and sinners as well.

Group or Community Deliverance

Your leaders must come together to take action.

> *Then the men of the city said to Elisha, "Please notice, the situation of this city is pleasant, as my lord sees; but the water is bad, and the ground barren." And he said, "Bring me a new bowl, and put salt in it." So, they brought it to him. Then he went out to the source of the water, and cast in the salt there, and said, "Thus says the* LORD: *'I have healed this water; from it there shall be no more death or barrenness.'" So the water remains healed to this day, according to the word of Elisha which he spoke. (2 Kings 2:19-22).*

From this text we can see that a location can be cursed to be barren and so produce death in various aspects of life. If you are located ignorantly in such a place, you will have a lot of battles and struggles to go through before noticing success and prosperity.

When King Solomon was dedicating the temple in prayer, God responded as follows:

> *When I shut up heaven and there is no rain, or command the locusts to devour the land, or send pestilence among My people, if My people who are called by*

> *My name will humble themselves, and pray and seek My face, and turn from their wicked ways, then I will hear from heaven, and will forgive their sin and heal their land. Now My eyes will be open and My ears attentive to prayer made in this place. (11 Chronicle 7:13-15).*

The heavens are shut over some people, people groups and nations, because of their sin and idolatrous practices. Devourers are eating them up from various corners. God's protective eyes are removed from them and their prayers are not heard. It happened to Israel in the days of King Ahab.

> *And Elijah the Tishbite, of the inhabitants of Gilead, said to Ahab," As the LORD God of Israel lives, before whom I stand; there shall not be dew nor rain these years, except at my word. (1 Kings 17:1)*

This announcement marked the beginning of drought and death of vegetation and animals and famine in the land for three and a half years.

Steps to Take to Bring Healing

1) Remember the mercy of God as written in 2 Chronicles 7 where we had read as well as 1 John 1:9; "If we confess our sins, he is

faithful and just to forgive our sins, and to cleanse us from all unrighteousness."

The Lord is not slack concerning His promise, as some count slackness, but is longsuffering toward us, not willing that any should perish but that all should come to repentance. (2 Peter 3:9)

2) Remember: there is no hopeless situation

Shall the prey be taken from the mighty, Or the captives of the righteous be delivered? But thus says the LORD: "Even the captives of the mighty shall be taken away, And the prey of the terrible be delivered; For I will contend with him who contends with you, And I will save your children. (Isaiah 49:24-25)

"... but with God all things are possible" (Mathew 19:26)

3) Confess your sins, family sins and the sins of the community and the leaders of the Community you are dealing with and the matters concerning the community.

4) Bring quality genuine repentance before God. This involves practical turning away from the sinful and offensive acts. If you live with a concubine, move out. If you have stolen things return them, etc.. Destroy all evil alters, customs, cultures and practices.

5) Reconcile yourself or the land and the people back to God according to Colossians 1:20

For it pleased the Father that in Him all the fullness should dwell, and by Him to reconcile all things to Himself, by Him, whether things on earth or things in heaven, having made peace through the blood of His cross. And you, who once were alienated and enemies in your mind by wicked works, yet now He has reconciled. (Col. 1:19-21)

6) Speak healing into your life and circumstances. In the case of a Community, do the same thing. By prophetic prayers reverse the curses and evil trends and plant seed of success, prosperity and progress.

7) Establish and sustain a godly culture for your life and the community to sustain your freedom and God's presence.

8) Spiritually and physically dismantle every evil structure using Isaiah 44:24-26. Put a stop to festivals and traditions that honor the dead and the devil.

Thus, says the LORD, your Redeemer, And He who formed you from the womb:"I am the LORD, who makes all things, Who stretches out the heavens all alone, Who spreads abroad the

earth by Myself; Who frustrates the signs of the babblers, And drives diviners mad; Who turns wise men backward, And makes their knowledge foolishness; Who confirms the word of His servant, And performs the counsel of His messengers; Who says to Jerusalem, 'You shall be inhabited,' To the cities of Judah, 'You shall be built, 'And I will raise up her waste places".
Isaiah 44:24-26

9) Rebuild by the Word of God and prayer the broken hedges of your lives and that of the community. (Ecclesiastes 10:5).

   He that diggeth a pit shall fall into it; and whoso breaketh an hedge, a serpent shall bite him.

10) Rebuild your life and community with precious spiritual substances as Isaiah 58:12

    And they that shall be of thee shall build the old waste places: thou shalt raise up the foundations of many generations; and thou shalt be called, The repairer of the breach, The restorer of paths to dwell in.

Claim this promise for yourself, your family and your land.

CHAPTER NINE

ELDERS AT THE GATE by: EMEKA NWANKPA
Chairman of Intercessors for Africa

*T*he ideas set out in this paper were originally presented at one of the leadership workshops held during the 4th International Ministers/Christian Leaders Prayer and Leadership Conference tagged "Nigeria 2000". The conference, which held from January 9 – 12, 2000 was organized by Ministers Prayer Network in Port Harcourt, Nigeria. The major aim of writing this chapter is to train us up as leaders and show us our leadership roles in society. As ministers, we are supposed to understand that there are certain responsibilities God has given us in the city where we live. What we are dealing with here goes beyond what we do inside or within the church. I would like to emphasize this point so that we understand the basis and thrust of this paper. It is supposed to train up leaders and ginger us up sufficiently to assume our leadership roles where we live whether as deacons, elders, evangelists, lay leaders, prophets or pastors. It is supposed to bring us to the awareness of who we are, and our responsibilities to society.

For this reason, our focus as leaders must reach beyond what we do inside the church, so that we can begin to grasp what leaders in the church must do for God on behalf of the general society. The background for our topic is laid out in Deuteronomy 21:1-9.

> *If anyone is found slain, lying in the field in the land which the LORD your God is giving you to possess, and it is not known who killed him, then your elders and your judges shall go out and measure the distance from the slain man to the surrounding cities. And it shall be that the elders of the city nearest to the slain man will take a heifer which has not been worked and which has not pulled with a yoke. The elders of that city shall bring the heifer down to a valley with flowing water, which is neither plowed nor sown, and they shall break the heifer's neck there in the valley. Then the priests, the sons of Levi, shall come near, for the LORD your God has chosen them to minister to Him and to bless in the name of the LORD; by their word every controversy and every*

assault shall be settled. And all the elders of that city nearest to the slain man shall wash their hands over the heifer whose neck was broken in the valley. Then they shall answer and say, 'Our hands have not shed this blood, nor have our eyes seen it. Provide atonement, O LORD, for Your people Israel, whom You have redeemed, and do not lay innocent blood to the charge of Your people Israel.' And atonement shall be provided on their behalf for the blood. So you shall put away the guilt of innocent blood from among you when you do what is right in the sight of the LORD.

As you read carefully these scriptures, please record your observations and questions. Use them for discussion with others within your church, fellowship or prayer group. Help to spread the message and by so doing, raise other elders for other cities around your nation.

Deuteronomy 21 verse 7 emphasizes on the expression,

"They shall answer and say, our hands have not slain this blood".

A careful look at that statement shows us clearly that it is aimed at putting away the guilt, which naturally stalks the lives of people in communities that have shed innocent blood. I want us to get a totally new and different orientation concerning the Bible, which was written not only to prepare us to go to heaven, but also to instruct us to live on this earth, enjoying abundantly the things which have been freely given to us according to God's perfect will. If you read this portion of the Bible carefully, you will come to the following inescapable conclusions: That God gave clear regulations to the children of Israel concerning how to deal with blood guiltiness in the society. Interestingly, this is not in the synagogue, not in the temple but in the city. Note the three times in that scripture you come across the phrase "elders of the city" and that what they were supposed to do was to be done outside; that the elders and leaders of any city in the world ought to know that they are responsible to God for crimes like murder, which are committed in the city where they live.

Death in the City

The first thing we must realize in dealing with this issue is that when such things happen, there is an effect of the murder, of blood guiltiness on the society. Many of us do not know, for instance, that if somebody is killed say, in the City of Port Harcourt, for whatever reasons, there are ripples that follow that deliberate act. When that happens, it is not just that somebody died, or that somebody was sacrificed; the blood of that person has an effect on the city and its inhabitants. Even as a Christian, the ripples affect you all the same. It does not really matter whether or not you knew anything about the crime or participated in the act. That is not what God is asking; the dead man's blood is surely bound to affect the society and the entire city because life is so vital and so precious. The elders at the gate or the leaders of any city are the pastors, the deacons, and other mature Christians who are opinion leaders, policy makers, proven servants, whose lives affect society in specific ways.

I know there are those who are by law charged with the responsibility of protecting people but that does not remove spiritual responsibility from the shoulders of knowledgeable leaders in the church towards (i) God and (ii) concerning the society. One of our problems in Nigeria (and I do not want to blame anybody for this shameful ignorance) is that we do not know enough of the Bible. Everything written in the Bible is supposed to help us at work, at home, in the office, in the city, in the community, to make our country a better place to live and work, a place to be proud of and to defend, if need be with our blood.

Another problem we have in Nigeria today is that we do not apply Biblical principles in what we are doing. Our governments, institutions, even the large majority of churches and families are not carrying out their affairs according to the pattern set down in the scriptures. To begin with, we must realize that God is not just the God of the saved. He is the God of everybody. So if any person is found slain, whether he is mad, poor, maimed, whoever he is, if he is found slain in the land, and it is not known who slew him, the bible specifies in the Old Testament that those concerned should go out and measure the distance, the elders of all the cities in the vicinity of the crime were meant to come out and deliberate over the matter and take appropriate action. The blood of Jesus cleanses much more than the cleansing of the ashes of the red heifer. But do not take God for granted. Let us take these things back to Him in prayer (Deuteronomy 21:8).

1) **Show Interest in Happenings in Your City**

   The first point to note therefore is that whenever any man is killed in our city, the elders must arise and show enough concern to take the necessary steps for atonement to free the city and its inhabitants from blood guilt. Let the elders "come forth" or "go out" as the New King James version puts it, and put their heads together regarding what to do to solve the problem. In Deuteronomy 21: 2-3, the bible spelt out what the city elders where to do in Israel: "Your leaders and judges are to go out and measure the distance from the place where the body was found to each of the nearby towns".

2). **Take Responsibility to Cleanse the Land**

   Please note carefully that the elders were not absolved from blame just because they could not uncover the identity of the criminal.

Regardless of this, they took steps to make atonement. They did not just ignore the corpse and the crime because they did not know who the culprits was (Deuteronomy 21:2). Someone has to take responsibility and from the statement I have just made, God expects us to take individual responsibility for what is happening around us. You can do this in your yard, in your line of shops, in that office complex, or company where you work. Take charge in the spirit realm concerning whatever is going on there. You are supposed to be the eyes, the ears, and the mouth of God in that place.

It is very unfortunate that we have been trained not to worry about what happens around us. We have been taught for many years to just come to church, give our offerings, be good Christians without making much difference in the societies where we live. That is not Christianity. When we live our lives in ways that do not give us the opportunities to impact our world and bring about transformation of individuals and our societies, we are wasting kingdom time and the potentials we have been loaded with. Satan who propagates this view knows what he is doing. He wants to reduce those who buy his lie to helpless tenants in the land.

3). Declare Your Innocence.

What does it mean to take responsibility? It means taking steps to correct mistakes, standing up for righteousness, speaking out when there is a need. When you boldly assert yourself in this way, you will begin to understand the power that God has given to you. If you wait for every member of the church to have an opportunity to preach, you will probably have to wait till the day Jesus Christ comes. You will discover, apart from what you do within the four walls of the church, that you are to act where you live and that is why Jesus said that you are the salt of the earth and the light of the world. Not just because of what we have inside us, but in terms of what we are supposed to do in the society, so that the will of God is protected. Notice here in Deuteronomy 21: 7, God says "they shall answer and say, "our hands did not shed this blood". The elders of the city had to say this so as to absolve themselves of bloodguilt. By so doing, they declared their innocence and spoke to all creation to free them from sanctions; they and other inhabitants within their cites. Theirs is the responsibility to speak to God, denying their knowledge of the murder and even who the man is does not absolve them of blame. They will speak to God also saying, we know that you created this man, we know that the cry of his blood is getting to your ears… They shall answer, "We did not shed this blood nor have our eyes seen it". The fact that we did not shed the blood, never saw it, or know who did it, does not mean that we have washed our hands off. We have a responsibility towards God and other inhabitants of the city, to cleanse the land of defilement. The lesson here is this, whenever anyone is killed, there needs to be atonement for people in the city, so that blame for that innocent blood is not laid at the feet of the elders of the vicinity nearest to that city and its people.

As an individual Christian leader, you need to discuss with God what is going on in the city.

You see and hear a lot through the electronic and print media. Go discuss with God in prayers. You are responsible! It might sound strange but that is the scripture, the truth we must internalize. They become relevant when you discuss this matter as soon as they threaten to happen, not after they have happened. Otherwise things get out of control. That is why today, despite the ever-expanding church population, and all the illusions of power church leaders seem to wield in their fancy organizations, we seem totally powerless to impact our cities for good. This is because we are not taking up our responsibilities of being the salt of the earth and the light of the world. Let us pay attention to the things, which happen around us. Let us sit as elders at the gates of our cities, communities, houses, markets and wherever we work, so that we can discuss all matters with God.

The gates are where major decisions affecting our cities and people are taken. If you are known at the gate, then you become effective as a legislator in the city. At this point, I would like to ask you to take some time to reflect on the importance of the Lord's prayers. *"... **Thy will be done on earth as it is in heaven...**"* That is what God wants. The way His kingdom comes is when His word is applied to society, when His word is used in government and its institutions, etc. And what is the will of God in this matter? It is that the blood of the slain should not be put to the charge of the people. Let us not forget that God the Father of our Lord Jesus Christ, the God of the church is also the King of the nation. In Deuteronomy 21:18 – 21, the scriptures speak of the elders' role in administering punishment.

4). Punish All Disobedience

Let me make one more point about crime, a matter that is gradually affecting almost all that goes on in society. It is our responsibility and we ought to discuss these things with God and exercise our responsibility from God concerning these things, because that is why we are elders at the gate. Deuteronomy 21:18-21 clearly directs that the father of a rebellious, gluttonous and hard-drinking son who has become a disgrace to his family and a public nuisance should be handed over to the city elders to be disciplined. If we do this, our cities will not suffer so much violence arising from drug addiction and alcoholism. The emphasis in this passage is *so that you shall put away evil from among you, so that all Israel shall hear and fear.* This is a matter of discipline. This scripture is a bit difficult to apply to our situation but can still be applied. You have young men and women who are rebellions, who are drunkards; they cause problems in the society, in the family but the question is, who will bring them before the elders at the city gates? Do the elders at our gates have the courage to look into their matters and order the people to stone them to death, so that evil shall be taken away from the land?

Now there are two ways of applying this. The matter of those who cause problems in our society, who introduce evil into the larger society, is something the church, particularly the Ministers ought to be concerned about. If our ministers actually understood the scriptures in terms of being Elders, they will not spend up to 10 minutes being idle in the

Pastors office in the whole of one year. These are matters of discipline and there are two ways of dealing with them. Realizing that Jesus has paid the full price for sin by His death on Calvary, we need to bring constantly to God's people those who are perpetuating evil in the society for sanctions. This is because the evil assignments they carry out troubles the people. If 12-armed robbers arrive Port Harcourt today, they will trouble the entire city. And if in the university, cultists kill twenty students, it will trouble the whole society. These young people who are making the society uninhabitable ought to be disciplined by active elders in our cities. But because we do not know that it is our responsibility to take care of these things when we hear them, or see them, we ignore them. I want to sound a note of warning that we do this to our own peril. For it is our responsibility to reduce or minimize crime, we have an obligation to throw these miscreants out of the society. But because we do not do it, we live in bondage, our houses are barricaded inside and outside, more than even the prisons; some of us who can afford it buy dogs for security. You no longer want to go out in the middle of the night, for fear of armed bandits.

5). Addressing Evil in the Society

Have you heard some of the evil, which goes on in the schools to which you send your children? How many of your children have been maltreated by other children? (I have heard horrible stories such as tales of senior students savagely beating and wounding junior students; while others have even stabbed some students to death). Do not wait for it to happen to you before you start praying. That will be too late. When we begin to talk to God about these things, evil will be checkmated in our cities and sanity will return to our nation.

When my children were in secondary school, we prayed and saw in the spirit realm things going wrong in the school system. My wife physically had to go to a particular school to do prophetic action, to pray and break the power of demonic operations there because two of our children were in that school. When my daughter was in the university, students in one particular female hostel had terrible experiences with ghosts. The students were scared stiff as they saw inexplicable sights and heard strange noises. Needless to say they could not concentrate on their studies. Suddenly things would begin to move around in the hostel, causing paralyzing fear to come upon the students. The girls got frightened and packed out. My daughter knew exactly the prophetic action to take, which she did and cast out the ghosts and the hostel calmed down and the girls came back. People, some much older, others younger than her started coming to her for counseling. Why are all these? It is because the principle of dealing with evil as it affects people is what we have to discuss with God, not only as it affects our own household but our entire community and nation.

Did you ever stop to ask yourself this nagging question: What kind of world will our children live in? In primary schools, they are initiated into witchcraft, in secondary schools they are in cults, by the time they get into the university; a machine gun is in the house. In one university I was told how shocked people were when ex-cult members who gave their lives to Christ began to confess to people where they hid their cutlasses and machetes. Their parents would have sworn that there were no guns in their houses. Yet in the wardrobes in these same houses were hidden dangerous weapons secretly brought in by their own children. If things remain like this, what kind of world will your children live in? That is something we need to come to terms with. In 1960, when I was in secondary school, the highest punishment you could give a junior boy was to ask him to kneel down or go and fetch water. If the boys fought, then you ordered them to cut grass. No Student had the right to beat another then. Today school children regularly beat, use bottles, pour acid, or use cutlasses, axes, guns, dagger, on each other. And many parents have lost their children in this gruesome manner. The major reason for all this is because as churches began to multiply in size and numbers, we did not continually deal with the matter by talking to God, otherwise things would not have deteriorated to this level.

Dealing With Immorality

At this point, let us take a few paces back to the earlier points we made about elders of the city declaring innocence and strengthening the moral fiber of the society through discipline. In this instance, we are looking at the issue of moral chastity. Our reference is in Deuteronomy 22:13-21. This is a slightly awkward topic to discuss but God who created man and ordained marriage actually asked that these things be written, so we must discuss them openly. The aim in doing this is that the blight of sexual promiscuity, which is threatening to drown out good morals in modern society, can be dealt with. We must realize that the whole question of morality, of the foundations of marriage is very important to God. Are you aware that today some churches are suggesting that potential couples test for AIDS before they get married? You never know where your seemingly cultured and "spirit filled" brother or sister had been before they got born again. Now can you imagine, marrying someone infected with aids in the church and rightly consummating that marriage in sexual union after the wedding only to discover that this union has become the beginning of your end? That is why God who wrote the bible and who knew that these things would happen was concerned about morality in society.

Beware of Curses

If you understand the spiritual dynamics of sex, the medical people will tell you that if two persons have sex with each other, they come into contact with the spirits of five other persons each partner had slept with so that anything these other people had come into contact with could also be picked up by them. Spiritually the Bible says that every sin a man commits, is outside the body but the sin of fornication is inside the body. It hurts you. When fornication is committed, whether you use condom or not, you make contact through the sexual act with spiritual forces.

Do you know that spirits go through physical walls not to talk of condoms? In so doing you partake of a baptism of demons, free of charge. Demons are transmitted even if you did not pick up any sexually transmitted diseases. The sex act is the most powerful way of transmitting demons apart from the bloodline. The other point we must note is that when you look at scriptures, you will find out that God is very much interested in the foundation of the family. Consider the case of Abraham and Sarah, a couple who faced temptation on their way to Egypt. Abraham looked at his wife and said to her, "Because you are a beautiful woman, you have to help save my life by playing a smart game of camouflage, which I am going to introduce. Please say that you are my sister when we get to Egypt so that they will not kill me and take you away." It was thus announced that Sarah was Abraham's sister when they arrived Egypt.

The elders in the king's palace arranged to bring the latest arrival into the king's palace and ultimately into his harem and this they did not knowing that she was somebody's wife. God was put in an awkward situation. If that man had an affair with Sarah, that could have messed up God's plan. So God did two things. He restrained Abimelech from touching Sarah and closed up the wombs of all the women in the king's palace. When the truth was finally revealed to Abimelech, he meekly protested to God saying, "in the integrity of my heart I did not know she was Abraham's wife". God said, "I knew you did not detect it but I restrained you." That will show you how concerned God was about purity. He restrained the man even though he had no intention. God told him bluntly that "this man is a prophet, let Him pray for you, otherwise you are finished." Abraham prayed and the man and his household were healed. You never know the curse you bring on the larger family when you touch another person's wife. You do not know. You do not understand. Adultery is such a horrible thing that nobody should think about it. How does it apply to us in Nigeria?

At one time there were about 12,000 Nigerian prostitutes in Italy and most of them were reported to be from Delta and Edo states. People sold their houses to send their daughters abroad without knowing that the young girls were swelling the ranks of prostitutes abroad. Contractors even took over the "business". Their conduct in Italy was outrageous. They did not practice their prostitution in houses and hotel rooms only but under flowers, parks, and openly by the street corners. What a shameful thing! As elders, we must lead the people in repentance for this great abomination. At one time all the indigenous prostitutes in Italy declared a day to give sex freely to men because by their reckoning, the prostitutes from Nigeria had messed up the trade for them. All the African Ambassadors called the Nigerian Ambassador and asked him "why is it that your women are making all our women look like prostitutes?" Now they are coming back with AIDS. The ECOMOG soldiers are also coming back from Liberia with AIDS. At least this is clear from various reports in the newspapers. Who will get it? It could be your brother or your sister, even if it is second-hand. And that is why when it came to morality God gave us these laws. It is not preaching about it but praying about it to deal with the spirits, which work to ensnare people through immorality. Let us take a cue from the men of the city of Jericho, who were concerned about the situation in the city.

> *Then the men of the city said to Elisha, "Please notice, the situation of this city is pleasant, as my lord sees; but the water is bad, and the ground barren." And he said,*

"Bring me a new bowl and put salt in it." So, they brought it to him. Then he went out to the source of the water, and cast in the salt there, and said, "Thus says the LORD: 'I have healed this water; from it there shall be no more death or barrenness.'" So, the water remains healed to this day, according to the word of Elisha which he spoke". *(11 Kings 2: 19 – 22)*

Please note that the focus here is not the situation of the church or Christians or the amount of money in the church purse. The people were concerned about bad water in the city. They took steps to rectify things. And this is a challenge to us. Beyond complaining and blaming Government, how many of us have seriously prayed about the water situation, the power situation in the country? How many of us have prayed about the productivity of the land? Do you notice that the prophet was operating in the city not in the temple nor prophesying to millions of his followers and asking for big tithes and offerings, to be promptly paid into the coffers of the church or fellowship? He was in the city giving out prophecies, which affected both believers and unbelievers alike.

Healing The Cursed Land

In his days Hiel of Bethel built Jericho. He laid its foundation with Abiram his firstborn, and with his youngest son Segub he set up its gates, according to the word of the LORD, which He had spoken through Joshua the son of Nun. 1 Kings 16:34.

What do we see here? The elders of the city of Jericho were alive to their responsibility. They took note of the disturbing facts:

(1) Their water was bad

(2) Their land was barren, and

(3) The people were sad.

But they did not know the genesis of the matter which could be traced to Joshua 6:26.

> *Then Joshua charged them at that time, saying, "Cursed be the man before the LORD who rises up and builds this city Jericho; he shall lay its foundation with his firstborn, and with his youngest he shall set up its gates."*

After the battle of Jericho, Joshua cursed the city. By the time the man who rebuilt Jericho finished the cursed project, all his children had died, 1 Kings 16:34. Unknown to him a curse was upon the city.

How many of us have ever bothered to find out if there is any curse on the part of the city or the area in which we live? What about the community we come from or our families? What is the history of that land on which your church is built? Some of us do not even know the family that sold the land to us. What was their background? The land could be under a curse. In the case of Jericho, somebody who had the anointing to tell the sun and the moon to stand still had placed the curse. And the curse was affecting everybody, believers and unbelievers alike; water was bad, women could not conceive, and the people did not know what to do.

Fortunately, the people were bothered to the point where they were forced to bring the problem to a man of God, to a prophet who came to stay in the city, because they were concerned about the city.

Many of us are so dead about our environment that we do not even bother with what is going on around us. As far as we can find a road to the church, a road to our house, a road to our shop and perhaps a road to our bank, that is all we care. The rest of the world can burn. If you are an "Island Christian", let me ask you this question, if there is a serious riot (in your city) will you be able to go to your church on Sunday? Note that what happens to the city affects everybody.

Because we are not taught that this Bible applies to everything, we do not know that God has given us the power to contend with *everything* that is going on in the society. You now know better. Put it into practice and see how God works it out because it works.

In the case of Jericho, how was the matter dealt with? The man of God needed salt. The people were prepared to do whatever needed to be done so that the matter could be resolved. Everybody was involved. They did the spiritual mapping, they knew what was involved, they brought the matter to the prophet who asked for salt and poured it into the water source and healed the land. To this day the sweetest oranges are grown in Jericho because the prayer of the man of God is still working. A man of God who had a double anointing was able to break the curse another man of God had put on the city. How does this work? By the application of wisdom; by the ability and willingness to get involved meaningfully enough in what happens in our cities, to take actions that count; actions that can affect generations yet unborn.

Just to illustrate this point, I would relate to you another story regarding the healing of a cursed land this time, in Malaysia. After our International Conference in Singapore in 1988 – in which I represented Africa, we went to Malaysia on a prayer assignment. In that country a lady missionary told us that the Port of Malaka used to be the busiest seaport in the world in the fourth century. It was by that reckoning also, the busiest in the whole of Asia. But the people prevented St. Francis of Assisi from preaching the gospel there. They threatened to throw him into a well, and they actually grabbed him and pushed him headlong into a well to press home their point. (I went to that well which is beside the Governor's house).

St. Francis of Assisi took off his sandals, cursed the city and left. That Seaport hitherto described as the busiest in the world tilted over and subsequently depreciated in value. Large deposits of sand covered the waters and closed down the seaport. Sand so filled it that as of 1988, if you wanted goods through the sea, you had to go fourteen nautical miles into the sea with barges to off-load the ship. Imagine what a curse will do to a city! Of course, it affected the economy, and destruction of business, import and export, and of course most other businesses closed, and we noticed that there was only one tiny road in the hitherto bustling port. We asked the Lord for direction, and He spoke demanding that the people repent of their sins against the man of God. The people did that at the well and after that He instructed us to go out to the sea. We walked along the sand bars, rolled up our trousers and walked into the sea. We prayed and poured salt into the sea, just as the prophet had done in Jericho. In 1998 when I went back to Malaysia, I was told that the town was doing well; it had a new airport. All kinds of things had happened to it. I even met a Chinese man who had bought a large piece of land there and had developed a huge estate. The town is now booming. The people do not even know what happened but that is the way God operates.

Any curse on a community can be broken. What it requires is finding out the reason for the curse, gathering together the people, pastors and intercessors and bringing repentance over the evil done in the land, and then God comes into the situation and you can carry out some prophetic action as the Spirit of God leads you.

It is not always compulsory that you use salt; you can anoint the place with oil and the curse will be broken. There will be a release and people will see the power of God. Prophetic action is not just putting money into the pocket of Christians. Do things outside, so that people can say "*this* is God in action".

The last case of healing and restoration we will consider in this chapter has to do with a family whose destiny was changed through relevant action by a knowledgeable elder in the land. The story is in the book of Ruth 4:11

And all the people who were at the gate, and the elders, said, "We are witnesses. The LORD make the woman who is coming to your house like Rachel and Leah, the two who built the house of Israel; and may you prosper in Ephrathah and be famous in Bethlehem.

Here we will go into details because there are many important lessons contained in the story which can instruct us. The story is about Ruth, the Moabitess and the mother-in-law, Naomi. This happened when Ruth and Naomi came back to Bethlehem of Judah, after the death of her children and husband. After Naomi had given Ruth instructions, directing her about the man who wanted to marry her, Ruth meekly and lovingly obeyed the wise counsel given by her mother-in-law, to the point of having a definite encounter with Boaz, who was clearly captivated by Ruth's beauty and grace. But there was a little problem. Boaz said, "There is somebody else before me. I need to go to the elders at the gate. I will see what they will say and what they will do. I will talk to the man who is supposed to have the right to inherit that particular piece of farmland before I can take a decision. Whatever he says, we shall do." When they got to the gate, the elders were there, and Boaz called the man and said.

"You know how our brother left and the condition of his widow who came back. You are supposed to inherit the property but if you are to do so, you will have to take his widow"

because this was the custom in those days. The man declined the offer and thus waived his rights and brought out his sandals to indicate this. Then Boaz stepped forward. The elders were at the gate to make sure things were done properly.

It is important for us to pray for things to be properly done wherever you are. Transactions such as buying land, building houses, properties, etc., must be done according to the word of God. **Many Christians get into trouble because things are not properly done. For example, when it is expected of them to do things in a proper sequence of say, steps 1,2,3,4 and 5, they do steps 3, 4, 5 only and leave out steps 1 and 2 thus leading themselves into difficulties.** We need Elders to direct us to do things properly according to the word of God. And when things are properly done, no man or devil can fault you. In our families it is our responsibility to make sure things are properly done, so that nobody attracts a curse, which will affect everybody.

Elders At The Gates

Elders At The Gates

QUESTIONS AND ANSWERS

Question

With reference to Deuteronomy 22:13 −21, what happens to the man who accuses a woman falsely?

Answer

In Old Testament times he was expected to pay a fine, in addition to paying the fine he had to marry the woman and not divorce her. He was not to be put to death because the woman needs a man to look after her.

Question

I come from a community where the Catholic Church thrives. There are not many believers there. How do I bring repentance to cause a turnaround from idol worship in this community?

Answer

Two or three believers can do the foundational work to deal with the root problem of idolatry. They must begin with prayers of repentance. Then they can dig out some information they need from knowledgeable elders and by the direction of the Blessed Holy Spirit. Keep a record as you begin to inquire about the foundation of that place. For instance, intercessors in Mexico found out that sixteen different Catholic churches in Mexico City are built upon former altars or shrines of the sun God. So, it is important to find out the roots of your community and what was done to set up the Catholic Churches there.

Secondly you need to take a fast and bring repentance for your community because of what they had done in the past. When you finish, ask God how to proceed. It may take some time but God will tell you what to do.

The same thing happened in Edda, a community in Eastern Nigeria. God had ministered to somebody who over a period of two years collected data concerning the origin of the place. He found out from his survey that the people had been worshiping a particular evil spirit for about five hundred years. When he finished, the Lord directed him to come and see some intercessors, who told him what to do. We sent ministers to Christians in that community who tutored them on land deliverance over a period of time. The Lord had instructed the intercessors involved in the project to carry out some prophetic actions, which involved their going round the community. After prayers, as they were about to leave for the march, they were intercepted by a 6½ foot long snake. All movement and singing stopped till somebody stepped forward and rebuked the snake in Jesus name. Immediately the snake rolled over and died with blood gushing out of its mouth. They dragged the dead snake into the church and celebrated for about an hour praising and worshipping God for giving them victory over Satan.

As they proceeded with the march all the seventy native doctors threatening resistance and who had sharpened their knives and were ready for the kill were super-naturally arrested. Unnaturally and inexplicably, they all fell fast asleep with their knives beside them. And by the time the believers had finished their prophetic action, one of the oldest priests/native doctors gave his life to Jesus. God showed himself in tremendous ways and a lot of things happened; people submitted to Jesus Christ, others handed over a lot of things to be burnt. The tabernacle of worship where the idol was worshiped was made of starch. During the civil war, troops of the Nigerian Army could not burn it because flammable substances like petrol and Kerosene employed in so doing could not respond. The Lord instructed that it be defiled. Two rules governed operations at the shrine:

1. No woman could enter there, and
2. Nobody could pick up anything that dropped within the vicinity of the shrine.

The Lord gave instructions that the shrine be defiled, and this is how the brethren went about defiling the evil altar and the grounds surrounding it.

They got a sister into that place, who dropped a Bible and promptly picked it up, again. They did all that and 2 weeks later fire came down from heaven and consumed the altar, without any human interference. Therefore, take your time, team up with other Christians and bring quality repentance before the Lord concerning your land, renounce all these things and the Lord will give you victory.

Question

There is an idol in my community called Umunne. When the chief priest died, his son who is a civil servant refused to step into the office. He handed it over to an elderly man in the family. When the Chief Priest's son retired from his government position and came back to the village, he still refused to take up the office, so the deity killed him. When the incumbent chief priest died no one in the family agreed to take up the office. The deity has now started killing people in the family periodically. So what do I do?

Answer

A Christian in that family has to bring true repentance before the Lord, first for the covenant with the deity and secondly for the priesthood office in the family. Next, call the elders together and minister the gospel to them from the point of view of highlighting the evils of idolatry. When they really understand from the biblical perspective how God sees idolatry and what it does to a people, some will repent. As a result, an avenue for deliverance will be secured.

Let us illustrate this point with a concrete example: A family somewhere in Anambra state in Eastern Nigeria served a deity called Okwuoma. When the prayer team from Port Harcourt arrived, the entire family was gathered. Seven of the elders were men about 70 years old and above. There were also many other young men. There were quite a number of hard working young men who were not progressing and about 15 divorced young women in the family. After teaching them about idolatry from the Biblical perspective, one of the old men refused to cooperate with the deliverance team in the destruction of the shrine. He maintained that he could not bear to see or partake in the destruction of the deity in his generation. His argument as he confronted the rest of the family was that this was the deity their fathers bequeathed to them. A young man got up and challenged him saying, "My father is dead. When you die and go to the other side, what will you tell our dead fathers about us? I would rather die if that will set this family free". That broke the spell. All the family members present broke down and began to cry rolling on the floor of the family house where the meeting was being held. Even the recalcitrant old man repented. A particular young man who had walked in and out of the venue of meeting smoking and generally trying to distract everyone from concentrating suddenly fell down at the feet of the ministers in the deliverance team and began to groan as if in pain. Thereafter, he took them to his shrine, in one part of the compound. It took two full loads with a Pick-Up van to clear the charms from the shrine including those dug from the walls of the house and that family was delivered. It took about five hours for fire to burn that shrine. Therefore, if you pray tenaciously and bring quality repentance before God for your family/community, there will be solution as your prayers get to the heart of God.

Question

I belong to a church which is about thirty years old. This church tends to pull down (in diverse ways) any pastor who wants to bring revival to it. There have been many revelations about the church. The major one speaks of a pit in the middle of the church. What do you think we can do to solve the problem?

Answer

What kind(s) of prayers have you been praying thus far? Did you bring repentance before praying? Did you find out who dug the pit? What does the pit represent? Your prayer must have direction for it to be effective. Until you find out all these things you cannot really deal with the sites and whatever lies buried underneath the earth in that particular location. A pastor had a problem. In a dream, he found twelve elderly men sitting on thrones as he came into his church. On inquiry he told them he was coming to his church to pray, but they told him to get out, insisting that they owned the place. When he came to me, I advised him to make inquiries about the foundation of the church, especially what was originally done on that site.

Result

The result of the enquiry shocked this minister. He found out that the land used to be a place of sacrifices and the original owners of the land were still holding things in trust for forces of darkness. Repentance had to start from there.

And all that was dealt with and eventually this pastor's breakthroughs came as God intervened to deliver the church.

One of the things about us in Pentecostal circles is that we are too much in a hurry to pray without understanding what we are praying about. We bind, loose, command, cast out perceived demons in utter ignorance. But the legal basis for which Satan is in a place must be dealt with before prayers are offered. Otherwise, our prayers will avail nothing. The first thing Jesus as well as John the Baptist spoke on was repentance.

Look at the experience of David, "the man after God's heart." He faced three years of famine during his reign as the king of Israel. God definitely did not want to put David to shame, but there was a problem, which needed to be uncovered and properly dealt with. David inquired and was then told about Saul and his "bloody house" (Saul had killed the Gibeonites) and David then knew what the problem was. First deal with foundations before making the next move. Save yourself unnecessary headache.

Question

Where I work, occultic influences are used to intimidate, manipulate and suppress people. How do I deal with this oppression?

Answer

Get together other Christians and discuss the issue. Begin by spiritually raising an altar, establishing the presence of the Lord Jesus Christ there. Secondly, deal with your own sins. Then bring identificational repentance concerning the office and your department before the Lord. That is, identify with the department as you confess the sins of all the officers who serve there up to the top. This genuine repentance involves your standing in their place and confessing from a broken and contrite heart all the things they are doing as though you did them. This is precisely what Daniel and Nehemiah did. Note that if there is no regular prayer, no quality repentance and no incense to stoke the fire on the altar in that place, the enemy will walk all over everything and everybody.

Agree with all other committed Christians in that place and pray a prayer of repentance. Stay on that for a season and do nothing else till God is satisfied and begins to give further instructions. When He says, "move to the next phase," then you do. You will discover that step-by-step, you will reverse everything that has been done there. Also you will need to deal with the satanic priesthood, the altars, and the words (these include the sanctions and litigations) they have spoken. Why? This is because they are potent.

In 1991, we got into Ethiopia from Kenya. Mengistu Haille Mariam was in Power. There were seven of us from different parts of the world. The Lord told me to inquire about the names of those who brought communism into Ethiopia. They gave us these names including the man called Menelike, I asked the Ethiopians to bring repentance before God concerning this whole thing and this they did. The next day the Lord said to me, speak into the heavens and blot out the voices of these men. Then the next thing the Lord asked me to do was to go to seven places in the city and pray. This I did quietly without anybody knowing. I went up to the fourteenth floor of a restaurant overlooking the presidential villa, and prayed. I went to the town square, the trade union complex, the Orthodox Church and a few other places in Addis Ababa and prayed. I went to the statue of Lenin, the Economic Commission for Africa, the OAU hall, all the strong places, and prayed, and within three weeks the government of Mengistu fell. Christians have so much power, but you find out that in many cities Christians are held like birds in the cage; prisoners in their homes and tenants on their own God-given land because of lack of unity and focus in the church. That is why those who know feel like bursting with anger and frustration seeing the useless and empty pranks believers are playing. Let us arise from this deadly slumber and cry to God to help save our land.

CHAPTER 10

City Eldership And Prophetic Presbytery
By: Ben Uduak Udofia
A Leaders of Intercessors for Nigeria

*F*or a background to this study, let us read the following scriptures: Deuteronomy 12; Numbers 24; Ruth 4: 1-11, Deuteronomy 22:13-20, Proverbs 31: 23

If you look at the Old Testament pattern of town planning, there were gates at the cities. If we go through various scriptures, we will discover that the administration of justice was done at those gates. Deuteronomy 21: 1–9, 19-21. In Ruth chapter 4 and Numbers 24 as well as Deuteronomy 22: 13-20, you will notice that it was these elders who spoke out on issues of sexual immorality, the importance of upholding the sanctity of marriage, chastity and family life. We will notice also that as I mentioned in Ruth chapter 4 and Proverbs 31, commissions, transactions were also carried out at the gates. In 11 Kings 2: 19-22, issues about the welfare of the city were decided at the gates and in Judges 9: 1-6, the choosing of leaders and many other things were done at the gates. But you will notice that, the watchmen on the walls of the city were the ones who directed the elders as to when to open the gates. I believe that if the Holy Spirit is at work in the elders at the gate, as in Christian leaders in the church, those leaders will be counted among those that we call full time or part time ministers. The thing with these elders at the city gate was the level of responsibility and authority of this eldership

These city elders were responsible for the welfare of the city. For instance, before Elisha could reverse the curse on the city of Jericho, there was this elder that went to Elisha to complain about what had happened in the city. Read Jeremiah 1: 9 – 12

"Then the LORD put forth His hand and touched my mouth, and the LORD said to me:" Behold, I have put My words in your mouth. See, I have this day set you over the nations and over the kingdoms, to root out and to pull down, to destroy and to throw down, to build and to plant." Moreover, the word of the LORD came to me, saying, "Jeremiah, what do you see? "And I said, "I see a branch of an almond tree." Then the LORD said to me, "You have seen well, for I am ready to perform My word."

Now we have just read the scripture in Jeremiah chapter 1, where we see that God gave Jeremiah His words and said Jeremiah was going to "root out" to "pull down", to "throw down", "destroy", and then "build" and "plant". In Jeremiah 1:11, we see where God speaks to Jeremiah asking him, "what do you see"? Jeremiah described what he saw, the branch of an almond tree, which speaks of the power of resurrection. That is the first tree to blossom after winter. Then the Lord said to him, "I am getting ready to perform my words"; that is, about pastors and ministers.

In Isaiah 55: 10-11, the Lord Almighty spoke clearly saying that the word that comes out of His mouth shall not return to Him void, but it shall accomplish the purpose for which it is sent. The first thing I want us to note is that there is creative power in the word of God. And secondly, I want us to know that we are God's mouthpiece on the earth.

The Earth is created for Men

When we talk about the issue of city eldership and the prophetic presbytery, we need to know that the earth was created for man and not for spirits. Spirits only have access to the earth through men. Thus, whatever happens in the city, whether good or evil is determined by men. If the men like you and I, and the women cannot take responsibility before God in the city then whatever the agents of the enemy want for their master, the devil will prevail in the city and that is what has been happening in our cities all along. We are very late in realizing this but thank God that we have at least woken up from slumber. If we become serious even with our feeble efforts, acting on the present knowledge we have, we can be sure that the zeal of the Lord will perform this thing. We have the responsibility of harnessing the immense power of city eldership before us. We have to affect the way people play politics and carry out their businesses even in the market. In politics, commerce and industry, people try to find out who should succeed them. We can, using superior legislation through the blood of Jesus, invite God's righteous ordinances in the cities, before people in the occult make ordinances on who should or should not prosper. And it is one of the responsibilities of city eldership and a sound prophetic presbytery to bring the counsel of the Lord to bear on the way things are done in our cities. We must note very carefully this point. Except we get the counsel of the Lord correctly, we will only get to a certain level in life and find out that we cannot go beyond that, even in business. There is a certain amount of money that Christian businessmen have not touched and this has to do with the tyranny of the kingdom of darkness. When we talk about city eldership and prophetic presbytery, one of the things we should know is that apart from the creative power of the spoken word of God, we are also God's mouthpiece on the earth, we must work to fulfill our destiny. Destiny is corporate. You cannot fulfill your destiny alone. It is when we invest what God has put in our lives in others, that we can fulfill our destinies better.

The first thing we are here for is the salvation of the nations (Galatians 3:29).

And if you *are* Christ's, then you are Abraham's seed, and heirs according to the promise.

Remember God gave Abraham a promise to be a blessing to nations. This promise is being fulfilled on earth in every nation for as many as come to God through Christ Jesus. We also are carriers of this blessing (in Jesus Christ). We should be able to bring people into their inheritance in God. When we talk about City eldership and prophetic presbytery and the fact that the earth was created for man, not for spirits, we must let the meaning of these words sink into us. It is the responsibility that man takes in the spirit realm that affects what happens on earth. Note Jeremiah 1:10 - 11, "with the words I give you, you will throw down, pull down, root out…" But after the fall of man, he needed to retain his God-given inheritance through offerings and sacrifices. In Genesis 4:8-10,

> *Now Cain talked with Abel his brother, and it came to pass, when they were in the field, that Cain rose up against Abel his*

> *brother and killed him. Then the L*ORD *said to Cain, "Where is Abel your brother?" He said, "I do not know. Am I my brother's keeper?" And He said, "What have you done? The voice of your brother's blood cries out to Me from the ground.*

When Cain slew his brother; the first thing that happened was that the earth took record. It opened its mouth and took the blood of his brother. And because of that, God said that the earth would not yield its increase. There are certain ordinances God has laid on the earth and there are certain things people do and the earth vomits them out.

Sacrifices and offerings are acts of the priesthood that make people regain their inheritance Hebrew 5: 1-3

> *For every high priest taken from among men is appointed for men in things pertaining to God, that he may offer both gifts and sacrifices for sins. He can have compassion on those who are ignorant and going astray, since he himself is also subject to weakness. Because of this he is required as for the people, so also for himself, to offer sacrifices for sins.*

A priest is somebody chosen from among men to make sacrifices on behalf of other people so that they can go into their inheritance in God. The first thing Noah did immediately after coming out of the ARK after the flood was that he built an altar to God.

Then Noah built an altar to the LORD and took of every clean animal and of every clean bird, and offered burnt offerings on the altar. (Genesis 8: 20)

An Altar is a meeting point between human beings and spirit beings and through them spirits gain entry into the earth. Altars represent gates in the realm of the spirit. When Noah built this altar to the Lord, he made himself as a priest relevant to the land and brought it into the covenant he had with God. God responded to the covenant and the first thing He told Him is about seedtime and harvest time. Of all things said, only these depend on man.

> *And the LORD smelled a soothing aroma. Then the LORD said in His heart, "I will never again curse the ground for man's sake, although the imagination of man's heart is evil from his youth; nor will I again destroy every living thing as I have done." While the earth remains, Seedtime and harvest, Cold and heat, Winter and summer, And day and night Shall not cease." (Genesis 8: 21 – 22).*

When we talk about city eldership, we must also be concerned about what we are sowing into the land and what are we going to reap. What are we sowing into the lives of people? Are we building men or are we building structures? Are we building people that can be in touch with heaven? Are we in touch with the prophetic unction of the earth, so that we can affect the realm of the spirit and effect changes in the physical? Take note that in Noah's days, one of the things men did was to gather together and attempt to build a tower that will reach into the heavens. By the power of agreement, they could have succeeded but for God's intervention.

God scatters them and picks Abraham, who goes to a new land and raises an altar to him. The second time he raises a territorial altar between Bethel and Ai. He pitched his tent and called upon the name of the Lord.

In Genesis 28: 11-22, Jacob, his grandson had a vision on that same altar of angels ascending and descending. He called the place the gate of heaven because man could access God from there. God created the earth and gave to man to rule and have dominion. Even after man failed, God had to come back to the earth as man. Even after that, He still promised the comforter. He needed man's consent and total agreement, that is why the disciples prayed till the Holy Spirit came. Without that, we cannot be effective in our eldership. God wants us to be effective in our spiritual legislation because it is the priesthood that determines the inheritance.

In Jacob's case, God stood on that ladder and spoke to him, giving him an everlasting promise, because of Abraham's covenant with God on that land. The angels who came now saw that territory as belonging to God. Because of the altar that was raised in Genesis 12: 7-8, God promised to redeem the inheritance. If that altar were not raised unto God, the people would have forfeited their inheritance. Before we even talk about city eldership, we have to deal with the priests so that we can understand the witness of creation. Whenever people mortgage their inheritance to powers, they forfeit the inheritance. If Abraham had not raised an altar to God, that place would have been a gate of hell not a gate of heaven. This is the main thing that Jesus raised the church to do, to deal with the gates of hell. Demonic spirits, which come from hell through the gates into a place, into a city, disinherit the people, they bring all kinds of troubles, violence, death, diseases to that locality. The bible talks about an agreement in cities where powers rule with human beings who are in covenant with hell. All over the world, you see that the Normans and the Anglo-Saxons, drove away the natives because of the satanic priesthood. In the United States of America, you observe that the native Americans, the Red Indians, the Mayans and those who had been there longest are even poorer than the people who came later from other places, the people who came from Europe and other nations and civilizations that had to do with God are the people you find in the embassies. And yet the Bible says in Isaiah 61: 5 that when you become the priest of the Lord, that the sons of the alien will be your plowmen and your vinedressers. When a child is born, many rituals are done and the child is dedicated with his umbilical cord to evil powers, the evil powers continue to hunt and influence that child. Even if you build a refinery in that place and make that child the manager, he will still be sorrowful.

These are spiritual powers and it is only a proper city eldership that pleases God that can release the people into their inheritance. It is the goodness of God that brings people into their inheritance. It is a proper city eldership and prophetic presbytery that ushers people into their inheritance in God. Pray that God can use you to release people into their inheritance. God can also use you to call forth those things that be not as though they were.

The Lord Jesus said, "if you deny me, I will deny you before my father." He also said that a man's enemies usually are "they of his own household." Your problem is not other people but those things you have subjected yourself to. In talking about city eldership that brings about prophetic presbytery, let us take a look at the New Testament:

> *"He will also go before Him in the spirit and power of Elijah, 'to turn the hearts of the fathers to the children,' and the disobedient to the wisdom of the just, to make ready a people prepared for the Lord." Luke 1:17*

It is possible now that the Lord is restoring the prophetic unction of the church in the spirit and power of Elijah, to begin to see the heart of the fathers drawn to the children. The city eldership must look at the restoration of fatherhood. The problem you and I have is that the proper structure of God's covering is not there in the church and without the proper restoration of God's provincial structure in the church; we cannot impact the nations with the power of God. We need a proper mandate and that mandate must be restored before we can move ahead. God can activate a corporate anointing on us by laying on of hands and by prophetic grace, unction and decrees, to activate in the lives of individuals, families and peoples those things which have been hidden in their lives by God, to make them a people great for the Lord.

To get to this level of city eldership, we must defend the concept of the territorial church. Is the church a place? No, the church is a people. Do we think that all that God meant is the current concept of the church? No, that is not likely. There is a need for us to begin to see how this grace can be impacted to others to raise up not only godly fathers but also sons. Our problem is the simple generational anointing, single pocket ministries. The next generation does not need to start their own revival. Our own generation should not just leave for the next generation an empty religion, ordinary desolation, but we should leave for them something that is created by the power of God. As fathers come, such as Eliakim just as God promised in Isaiah 22: 20-22,

> *Then it shall be in that day, That I will call My servant Eliakim the son of Hilkiah; I will clothe him with your robe And strengthen him with your belt; I will commit your responsibility into his hand. He shall be a father to the inhabitants of Jerusalem, And to the house of Judah. The key of the house of David will lay on his shoulder; So he shall open, and no one*

shall shut; And he shall shut, and no one shall open.

When he becomes a father to the city, he will give him the key of David, whatever he opens will be opened and whatever he shuts will be shut. That is the power we have as elders as we take up this responsibility before God. We now need a proper restoration of fathers. In the book of First John, these unique fathers are not just those who have been from the beginning but also those who know the word of God (1 John 2:1-14).

It is not possible to have the city eldership in a place where the Christians are non-dispensational. What is God's purpose now? What is the Spirit of God saying now? It is only those who know what the spirit of God is saying now that will overcome. Why do you think that John in this passage is talking about equipping, reconciling the fathers and the sons, equipping a people for ministry? Why is this passage referring to the spirit and power of Elijah? In the life of Elijah in 1 Kings 19, the Lord passed by Elijah to brood over him and impregnate him with a new vision. Elijah was coming to a new level of ministry where he would be able to birth a son. God told him after that to go and anoint two kings and anoint a prophet to succeed him. When we understand what God's prophetic counsel is and know that we are his mouth piece on the earth and gather together on the basis of what he wants done and begin to speak on the basis of that counsel, we can begin to internalize his counsel in our lives and impact our generation with it. Do we know the actual reason why we have problems of succession in ministry? Many people build ministries and when they die, that is the end of that ministry. Why? Partly because of greed, and a lack of the proper vision to raise successors whose allegiance is to God.

Right now, with all that God is saying about us taking a leading role in the move of God in Africa, we see that it will be important for the power of God to be properly handed over. We need to get to that level where we can move by the unction of the Holy Spirit to bring an opening of the communication line between the father, the sons and also an impartation of gifts to the younger generation. If the younger generation does not do greater exploits than we have done, then we have failed. Elisha had a double portion of Elijah's anointing. The anointing on Elisha was so strong that he did not need to kill Jezebel himself. He just imparted that anointing to one of the sons of the prophets. He did not even need to anoint Jehu. It was one of his boys that anointed Jehu. They consciously passed on the anointing of God on their lives from one person to another. We need to begin to pray to have an expansive personality in the spirit. Our problem is that our natural attitudes have affected us. Our prejudices, preferences and biases must begin to retire to the graveside, if we must move along with God.

We have not really been people that are transparently honest and open. God is calling for fruitfulness in this season. In the things of God, as you emerge from one level of grace to another, you will grow in what God is saying. When God spoke to Jeremiah He asked him saying, "what do you see"? Jeremiah answered and told God what he was seeing, and the Lord said, "l am watching over those words to establish them".

The Devil's Agenda

What is the agenda of the devil regarding city eldership and prophetic presbytery? According to Isaiah 14: 17,

> *Who made the world as a wilderness, and destroyed its cities, Who did not open the house of his prisoners?*

The devil wants to make the world like a wilderness. Where did he get that concept of the wilderness? In Genesis 1:2, when there was chaos on the face of the earth, the Bible records that the Holy Spirit was busy brooding over the earth and he is the one that gave life to the earth.

We have that same life of God inside of us by virtue of the Holy Spirit dwelling in us so that when we speak, things are created. We can speak into people's lives in a way that we can help them to be properly aligned and be helped to fulfill the destiny of God for their lives. The devil indeed wants to make the world like a wilderness, but we have been given a mandate to stop him.

> *"The voice of the LORD shaketh the wilderness; the LORD shaketh the wilderness of Kadesh."*

The wilderness is a place of sterility, but the voice of the Lord makes it to bear fruit. As we come into the counsel of the Lord and begin to seek him together and speak prophetically into the lives of people and situations, wilderness situations will become fruitful.

The voice of the Lord makes the wilderness to be no longer sterile. Look at the situation in your life. Is there anywhere you are not really fulfilling the mandate of God over your life or your congregation or territory? There is something wrong. But we are not helpless. We are God's mouthpieces on the earth. If we can only wait in the presence of God and incubate his counsel collectively as city elders, there is no entity we will speak into that will remain the same. Note that only the voice of the Lord makes the wilderness fruitful. When we speak God's prophetic word over a place, the Holy Spirit broods over that place to bring about fruitfulness out of any sterility in that place. On the converse side, God gets angry at a land and causes it to vomit a people when they are enslaved by idolatry, immorality and blood guiltiness.

Requirements

We must note that if we would operate effectively as a prophetic presbytery, we have to be holy, obedient and willing to pay a price. Those who operate in the office of Prophetic Presbyters on the basis of God's counsel and want God's kingdom to come down upon their lives must be willing to pay the price. They must patiently wait before God to receive His words concerning the situation in their cities and speak healing from the word of God to make the wilderness fruitful. The fate of our cities and communities and even our nation depends on us.

We are not giving God a proper platform to change the lives of our people and to affect their destinies. Unfortunately, the kingdom of darkness and their human agents are desperately doing all sorts of things to thwart this. They know what they are doing when they work towards bringing about cultural revival, in which they re-enact several kinds of satanic worship and sacrifice of blood to idols. When the ancient customs and traditions enshrined in these devilish festivals are organized and the public is invited to watch, responsible human beings go to watch these and come under the grip of these idols.

When we talk about city eldership and prophetic presbytery, we are talking about elders coming together to provide a godly covering for the people. Because of idolatry and blood guiltiness that is prevalent in our cities, there is a covering of darkness that is cooperating with the agenda of the devil to make the place a wilderness and impoverished. The missionaries that came with Christianity moved through the waterfront in the coastal areas to the hinterlands. How come these places are still looking so primitive, so underdeveloped and so deserted? It is because of a missing element, which is the voice of the Lord, which is also the element of God's prophetic counsel. When the elders in these places know this and start operating in their mandate, things will change. With their apostolic mandate, they will gather and say, "anyone's sins we forgive, and remit are forgiven and remitted and anyone's sins we retain are retained."

And God says that he watches over that word to establish it. The church is the entrance that God has, the power through which he can operate on the earth and affect things. In Matthew 16, Jesus said, "l am going to build my church and the gates of hell shall not prevail against it". The church is a legislative body at the local congregational level. At the territorial level, we come together, to agree that the kingdom of God will come and be established on earth and that the voice of the Lord should come into the land to begin to cause the wilderness to become fruitful, so that the people can be released to their destinies in God. This is the challenge before us.

How To Come Into The Office Of Eldership

Intending city elders must encounter the cross. How do we come into this office of eldership? The Bible says no man taketh this honor unto himself. To get into the Eldership, you have to encounter the cross and it must deal with every flesh in your life and deal with all the denominational and tribal sentiments in us. Then and only then will we qualify as city elders. We have attempted to do many good things together before, but we always ended up in factions. The awesome responsibility of making legislations through the instrument of city eldership is not done at the level of tribal sentiments but on the level of sacrifice. Why can't we easily practice city eldership here? Because tribalism comes from idolatry and the level of tribalism that exists in a place is determined by the kind of elders in that place.

For instance, Jeroboam built two altars in Dan and in Bethel. Because of those two altars, no prophet in the northern kingdom could hear God. When God wanted to deal with those altars, he sent for a prophet from the southern kingdom and a prophet from the northern kingdom arranged with the devil to kill this other young prophet. See how devastated the whole place was? For 424 years, the entire infrastructure was destroyed. No king could do well because of the false altars Jeroboam built. That's how powerful evil legislation can be. In the time of Christ, when he met the Samaritan woman at the well, she reminded Him that being a Jew had nothing to do with her, while she is a Samaritan. In other words, she was saying that there was no relationship between the two people. Supposing He had slapped that woman because of her idolatry? There would have been a fight.

Idolatry Makes A People Proud

They delude themselves in thinking that they are better than others. When you look critically with the eyes of the spirit into the fights in our communities, you discover that the bottom line is idolatry. Tribes and communities fight others simply because of the idols they serve and pay allegiance to. These idols want human blood. It is actually the queen of heaven in her thirst for blood that causes these fights. The blood is used as a sacrifice and a means of appeasement for the queen of heaven.

How do we rise to counter this? The Lord said, "l have put my words in thy mouth" and he said with these words we will "pull down", "destroy", "root out", and "plant" what God wants us to plant. To come into city eldership, these are the things we are called to do:

1). Be Conscious Of Your Environment

To come into city eldership before God, one has to be conscious of his environment. You need to be spiritually aware of your environment. Be knowledgeable about things around you. Ezra 4:15

> *That search may be made in the book of the records of your fathers. And you will find in the book of the records and know that this city is a rebellious city, harmful to kings and provinces, and that they have incited sedition within the city in former times, for which cause this city was destroyed.*

The challenge of the city eldership is how to bring a people to their inheritance. For each people God has a redemptive purpose. We should be able to study the history of a place and know why there are certain problems in the land. Jesus opened those books in heaven because He has been slain, and he redeemed us with his blood out of every nation, tribe and people and made us kings and priests to our God and we shall reign on the earth. We are saved to reign on the earth. We need to get to a point where we can make decrees that are binding.

2). Be Available And Committed To Corporate Prayers.

We must be able to meet and pray corporately. To get intimate with people, you must be able to meet together with them to pray. Let's see Acts 13. It is because of the fulfillment of Acts 13 that we are here today. After fasting and praying, they laid hands on Saul and Barnabas for impartation. What do city elders do?

They gather people together to pray and fast. As they pray, you share with them the burden of God for the land. You move them into repentance so that God can hear their cry and bring down a refreshing and a restoration. Then they lay hands on the people for impartation especially before they undertake specific community deliverance project. There is a scriptural truth about laying on of hands. The people you lay hands on turn out to be even better than you, because something happens to them in the realm of the spirit.

Leaders and Ministers must begin to realize that nobody manufactures anointing. The problem we have is that instead of laying hands and commissioning people and releasing them into their giftings and destinies in God, we sit on people. We should call forth a leadership that serves. When Paul was called, the spirit said to the apostles, "separate for me Saul and Barnabas unto the assignment unto which I have called them". But he later became Paul. You do not change a people by lording over them; you change a people by serving them. We in the church do not serve the nation. God's counsel in our mouth is to be used to serve the people and to serve the purpose of God.

The Lord said He would not do anything without revealing it to his servants the prophets, because what God wanted done, would be done through his servants who listen to his voice. He said his word, which goes forth out of his mouth, has an ability to create. Therefore, we must squarely face the challenge of positioning people and commissioning them to take specific responsibilities.

3) Be Available For Regular Corporate Prayers And Fasting

This call is also task oriented. There are specific things that need to be done which we need to seek the Lord for and we need to seek the Lord to know who should do those things. The problem is that when people gather we often use our human assessment to say, "This person should be commissioned to do this assignment, or that person should be commissioned to do that". But here they were fasting and ministering to the Lord when they received directives from the God they serve. It is time to multiply. In the prophecy in Isaiah 54: 1-3,

> *Sing, O barren, you who have not borne! Break forth into singing, and cry aloud, you who have not labored with child! For more are the children of the desolate than the children of the married woman," says the* LORD. *"Enlarge the place of your tent, and let them stretch out the curtains of your dwellings; Do not spare; Lengthen your cords, and strengthen your stakes. For you shall expand to the right and to the left, and your descendants will inherit the nations, and make the desolate cities inhabited.*

God spoke to the barren to begin to rejoice and enlarge her coast for she is going to increase and her seed will inherit the nations and cause desolate cities to be inhabited.

4) Share Our Lives Together

As we come together, we do not only belong to the Lord, we belong to each other, so we pray and seek the Lord out of sincerity of heart and purpose, because we want his kingdom to come on earth. None of us wants to outdo the other person. We need God to bring to us that level of relationship where we share the life of God together. We are alive to fulfill a common purpose of God on the earth. God said he would watch over whatever we say to perform it. After Saul and Barnabas were prayed for, the first major encounter they had was with a sorcerer. No wonder Paul, filled with the Holy Spirit, spoke to this man and immediately what he said affected creation. The prayer of commissioning that he received was part of what enabled him to pray in such a way that things in the heavenlies were activated and in turn affected things on the earth.

We are called into city eldership, not just to meet, fraternize and eat and drink each time we gather for fellowship, but to carry out the functions of City elders. We are called into corporate fasting. If possible, arrange daily praying for the city in terms of prayer cells. Arrange corporate fasting, where people can seek the Lord sometimes for 30 days and sometimes 21 days and take up specific projects, maybe to deal with certain altars and spirits in the city. These are the things we are called to do. The major religion in the whole world, Islam, which is fighting against Christianity, controls the world through fasting. Did it ever occur to you to find out why the practitioners of this religious creed carry trays of suya on their head to sell; but they do not eat the suya as much as you do? Or why they are busy manipulating the heavens, facing the moon to pray and draw power from the sun? Realize that God has assigned the sun to rule by day and the moon to rule by night. They manipulate things in creation and gain wealth from the heavens. There is a lot of manipulation of wealth from the heavens.

Membership Of The City Eldership

The city eldership is not just for pastors alone. The body should be made up of Christian leaders. There should also be prophets and evangelists even in the market place. In the network, men such as prophets and apostles should be mighty Christian leaders in charge of education, people who are leaders in their communities. They come together to seek the purpose of God for the city, so that the life of the kingdom of God can influence everything the people do in their community. That is our greatest challenge. The school we went to and the things already happening in our communities were not based upon the principles of the kingdom but this is what we are called to correct as we pray to change the ordinances. It is also in this prophetic presbytery that we will proclaim a release of the captives from specific bondages.

Encouragement

No situation is hopeless. Moses, Mordecai, Esther, Nehemiah, Daniel and some others stood alone before God for their nations at one point or the other. When you do not have Christian leaders knowledgeable in this area, please don't sit down and cry. Get on your knees and begin to pray. Determine to stand in the gap for your city. Convene a meeting of people of like minds and begin something immediately. Your sun will soon shine full blast.

Where you have any queries, you are welcome to write to:

International office, Spiritual Life Outreach,
P. O. Box 7960, Port Harcourt, Nigeria
or mpninterheadoffice@yahoo.com.

REFERENCES

Webster, Merriam, Webster's Ninth New Collegiate Dictionary, 8th Edition, Springfield, Massachusetts, USA, Merriam Webster Inc, 1989.

Crudence, Alexander, Crudence Complete Concordance to the Old and New Testaments, Grand Repids, Michigan USA, Zondervan Publishing House, 1975.

HEAD OFFICE

3 Babbe Street, D/Line, P. O. Box 7960, Port Harcourt.

Tel. +234-(0)803-952-2243,+011-234-9079990000

Or

11 Benjamin Opara Street, Off OluObasanjo Road, GRA, PH.**Tel.** +234-907-999-0000, 0703-1694901, +011-234 - 8037298378

E-mail: mpninterheadoffice@yahoo.com

ENUGU

43 Zik Avenue, Uwani. Tel. 08037951172

UYO

15 Wellington Bassey Way (Barracks Road), Uyo. Tel: 07035335482

ABUJA CONTACT

Mrs. Ginigeme Erute Tel: 08035502661

Other books written by Dr. & Rev. Mrs Mosy & Chinyere MADUGBA

FOUR LEVELS OF SPIRITUAL WARFARE

There is constant war in the heavenlies over the souls of men, and the moment a man declares for Christ, the demonic world immediately reacts and marks him for an enemy who must be brought down, killed and destroyed. The only way out is to know how to fight back and still stands tall. This book shows you how.

IMPACTING YOUR WORLD

Impact is the unmistakable, undeniable significant or major effect on our environment or generation as a result of our existence. Your impact is a combination of the things that happen around you just because you exist. This book will help you to know how to be a positive impact maker. It is a must read for everyone who will make a difference in this world

MISSIONS THE GREATEST NEED OF THE HOUR

"David…a man after God's heart", is a very well known phrase in Christian circles. The secret was that he knew the one thing that gave God so much pleasure at that time and season, and he did not hesitate to do it. That was praise and worship. You can be the David of today, not just in making melodies unto God, but in getting involved in the one thing that pleases God most in this season. Discover what it is and how to do it right in Missions Now as Never!

BROKENNESS

In this very moving and inspiring book, the author identifies brokenness as an unavoidable ingredient in the making of the man that would be useful to God. It seeks to expose brokenness as the vehicle through which we can have a much more intimate, warmer and deeper relationship with the Lord.

APOSTOLIC LEADERSHIP

There is something far beyond the realm of human reasoning that could turn unknown, uneducated, unwealthy and unpopular men and women, unarmed with guns and switch blades, to an all-time catalysts and pillars of the unstoppable global church revolutionary transformational movement and succeed; "For they turned the evil world upside down", it is *apostolic leadership*.

APOSTOLIC WOMEN CAPACITY BUILDING TRAINING MANUAL

Capacity building means to increase the ability of an individual to function. As God moves His daughters to the frontlines, it is mandatory that they increase their capacities for growth, competence, leadership and excellent performance.

With this in place, they can progress beyond old limits set by culture, human traditions or even superstitions, and navigate successfully to the frontlines in the market place, corporate world, politics, church ministries and professions.

STEP INTO THE NEW SEASON
God is a God of times and seasons. He apportions times and seasons to everything He does on the earth. This book tells you where we are right now in God's calendar and how to position yourself to be relevant in it. Like the sons of Issachar who knew the times and what Israel ought to do, you will not only watch events happen but make them happen.

GOD'S AGENDA FOR WOMEN

The divine moment of women is here! According to God's divine agenda for women in this decade 2011-2012, a great prophetic window of opportunity has been opened before women all over the world to rise and become the best they can be in every area of life. An apostolic mantle has been released for them to become frontliners with the spirit of excellence. Get this book, read it meticulously, catch the holy fire that you need to get quickened in the Holy Spirit and proceed to make history and to rule your world.

FOUNDATION NECESSARY FOR A SUCCESSFUL MARRIAGE
Many people have written about marriage and truly much has been said about it. However, we have found this book "Foundation Necessary For Successful Marriage" in a class of its own. We are convinced that this book is not just one of those marriage books but a book whose contents came out of divine inspiration to those committed to the call of God on their lives. You need to read it!

UNDERSTANDING THE GROWING NEW PROPHETIC AND APOSTOLIC MOVE OF GOD

The new Prophetic and Apostolic season in which we live, calls for understanding to enable us function effectively in the Body of Christ. The book in your hands will take you from ignorance or your present level of understanding of God's move in this season to a deeper and higher level. It will teach you how you can develop the needed mindset to enable you flow relevantly and fruitfully with His Spirit.

UNDERSTANDING THE MINISTRY OF THE APOSTOLIC WOMEN
This book tells you who the Apostolic Women are and how you can get supernaturally equipped to become one. If you are a woman with this book in your hand, you are living in the best time for women in the history of the church on earth. Tap into it and get the best out of it.

PRAYER POWER

With this book in your hand and a willingness to be obedient to the call to prayer, you can rule your world. It explains what prayer is, teaches the process of growing strong in it and equips one with the knowledge of all the different types of prayer.

AFRICA'S TIME OF RECOVERY
As one of the keepers of the Gates of Africa, I announce to you the arrival of her restoration and empowerment season. This book contains lots of reliable prophetic words that could guide you to make the best out of this season in the history of Africa. Don't wait, read and act by the information contained therein.

THE JAEL COMPANY

This book shows you how you can use whatever you have to serve God in most spectacular ways like Jael will use a tent peg to kill an army general and bring to an end a national war.

KILLING THE MARRIAGE KILLERS
This book provides you with vital knowledge to build together a healthy, lively, fulfilling and highly productive marriage. Many marriages have been recovered, revived or restored by applying the principles shared in this book.

ELDERS AT THE GATE
This book shows you how to be an effective gatekeeper. It will help you turn your city around for good to God's glory. Your eyes will literally pop out as you read about God's dramatic miraculous interventions in the affairs of families, cities and nations. It also explains the reasons behind a few global puzzles that the secular world have no answers to. It is a very powerful resource. Go for it!

THE POWER OF NETWORKING
"No man is an island," so goes a popular saying and we are in an era of advancement through knowledge and information. Networking is inevitable in every field of endeavour today: computer, communication, the Airlines, even nations and governments cannot operate nor make progress on their own without linking up with others; neither can you as an individual survive alone in your chosen area of endeavour! Incredibly, God is the Author of networking! Find out how those ahead of you made it, and get challenged to excel above them and have an edge over your peers through this incredible book. A must-have and a must-read for every breathing human living in the 21st century! If married, it also touches some intricacies about marriage that most books avoid.

THE MATURE INTERCESSOR
This rich expose seeks to reveal some deep secrets and critical issues that make for successful, mature intercession. It is a giant step towards helping to raise the desperately needed, well trained, godly intercessors for today's church. It also attempts to expose the various perspectives that make up a mature intercessor.

This book gives you the right word to speak over every situation in your life and make you victorious in every conflict and prosperous in all areas of life. It is awesome.

APOSTOLIC WOMEN TRAINING MANUAL VOL. 2
Raising a competent company of well informed, equipped, furnished and inspired women, who can function very efficiently on the frontlines with the right spirit, is one of foremost goals of Ministers Prayer Network Apostolic Women Unit. This book is dedicated strictly to achieving the aforementioned goals. Keep it handy and study it.

GOD'S UNBEATABLE ARMY
This book will inform God's people about the characteristics of the Unbeatable Arm, its member mobilization, selection by elimination, training, equipping, and commissioning. You will have to make a choice at the end whether to join this army or not. However, it is a thrilling experience to be part of it.

WOMAN YOU CAN RULE YOUR WORLD
This book is written to take the limiting scales from off the eyes of Christian women so they can catch new visions, equip themselves with tools like a ladder, to enable them climb to the top and rule their world.

The time to start the journey is now. *"Good things come to people who wait, but better things come to those who go out and get them." (Anonymous).*

FRONTLINE INTERCESSION
Intercession can be ordinary and uninteresting if done as a routine and without much understanding. We can break the jinx to set a new pace for our generation. We need to come out to the frontline, get enlightened, get committed and develop stamina for the task ahead. The church earnestly needs righteous, powerful, fervent, consistent, reliable, selfless and revolutionary frontline intercessors in this season. This beautiful book will give you insight on how to enlist.

WOMAN OF GOD ARISE
The author pays great inspiring tribute to womanhood. Every woman who reads this book will have every cause to celebrate being a woman. In addition, it points out how to locate your *Kairos* times within your *Chronos* time and make use of the prophetic gate they open to you to excel in life.

THE GLORY OF WOMANHOOD
Women are very unique and special to God in many ramifications. They are the finest and crown of creation, and a major factor to be reckoned with. They are shakers and movers of the homes, church, society and nations. They are an embodiment of solution. A world without women is unthinkable. Womanhood is a great and high calling that can be quite exciting, fulfilling and rewarding. It is enhanced manhood. Women carry in them and around them glory worth exploring. This book will guide you on the interesting journey of pleasant discoveries, of the glory of womanhood.

WHEN WOMEN PRAY LIKE WOMEN
Read this book and discover what happens when a woman decides to stop competing with the man; looks inwards and takes her God-given place as a woman, and do things the God-defined woman way, especially in the place of prayer. Find out the amazing results in When Women Pray like Woman!

The Minister's Wife
The Minister's Wife is simply a heroine! She is a priceless jewel of inestimable value. This book will tell you more about her. Enjoy it!

DEALING WITH EVIL FOUNDATIONS
God's desire for ALL His children is that they may prosper (in every area of life), be in health, and be constantly connected to Him a tall order for most Christians! In Dealing With Evil Foundations, Rev. Madugba reveals by scripture, that the reasons for these setbacks might be from the spiritual condition of your roots (not the witch next door!) How high you go in God is determined by how sound and deep your roots are. You can break through to good success if you so desire.

ON FIRE FOR GOD
On Fire for God is one book that will move you to yield to the Holy Ghost's invitation to join God's fire carriers and help this present church to recover her losses of yesteryears and to advance to the much needed victory.

TRAINING TO LAST IN SPIRITUAL WARFARE
Warfares of any kind are rife with casualties. Every soldier knows this too well. But this should not scare you from enlisting in God's army; neither do you have to be a casualty or prisoner of war! This book teaches you God's safe and exciting ways of warring, while you have a good time out of it!

www.ingramcontent.com/pod-product-compliance
Lightning Source LLC
Chambersburg PA
CBHW050800160426
43192CB00010B/1583